The MY-FUN-WITH-WORDS

dictionary

by JAMES ERTEL

illustrated by GEOFFREY BRITTINGHAM
SEYMOUR FLEISHMAN
VERNON McKISSACK

published by THE SOUTHWESTERN COMPANY

Nashville, Tennessee

PRINTED ON RECYCLED PAPER

Design: Willis Proudfoot, Don Walkoe
Production: Robert H. Grigg

abcdefghijk**l**mnopqrstuvwxyz

ladder A **ladder** is a thing that helps you get up there so you can get the peaches off the tree. The pieces that go across on a **ladder** are called rungs. If you would rather eat radishes, you won't need a **ladder.** Radishes grow under the ground.

ladybug Not all **ladybugs** are **ladybugs.** Some of them are gentlemanbugs. **Ladybug** is a name we give to a kind of small beetle with round spots on its back. **Ladybugs** are helpful. They eat other bugs that harm farmers' crops.

lake It would be hard to water-ski in your bathtub, but you could water-ski on a **lake.** A **lake** is a largish body of water that has land all around it. A **lake** is larger than a pond. Some **lakes** are so big they look like oceans.

lamb No **lamb** has ever been known to attack a wolf, or anything else. A **lamb** is a young sheep. Everybody knows that **lambs** are gentle and friendly. When somebody says "Mr. Jones is a **lamb**," that does not mean Mr. Jones has four feet and a short tail. It means the person thinks Mr. Jones is gentle and friendly.

land Land is stuff you can walk on. Maybe it's dirt or rock or sand, but if you can walk on it, it's **land**. "This is my **land**," says your father. Maybe he means the piece of ground he owns or the country you live in. **Land** is very different from water.

lap When your mother stands up, her **lap** disappears. When your father is sitting down, he makes a **lap** you can sit on. The **lap** is sort of like a chair. When you sit down, you make a **lap** that can hold a puppy or a baby brother.

large "This is a **large** egg," you say. A three-foot egg is a **large** egg. A thing that is **large** is bigger than you thought it would be. Maybe a **large** dinosaur laid that **large** egg. Maybe you had better look behind you.

last If there is nobody in back of you when you finish the race, you are **last.** You are **last** if you are at the end of the line for the movie. It's not always bad to be **last.** Some people like to have the **last** word in an argument.

laugh You know how to **laugh.** When you think something is funny, you throw back your head, open your mouth, and make a "ha ha ha" or "ho ho ho" kind of sound. You feel good. Only people can **laugh.** Mice have never learned to do it.

lazy "My lion is **lazy**," says Lillian. "He doesn't want to pull my cart. He's a **lazy** lion." Someone who is **lazy** does not want to work, or is very slow about it. Get rid of that **lazy** lion. Get a horse.

lead If you are the one who marches in the front of the parade, you **lead** the parade. A **leader** is somebody who shows the way to the ones who follow him. It's a tough job to be a **leader.** If you **lead** the parade into a swamp, people will get mad at you.

learn When you first found out that ice is cold, you **learned** something. You **learn** by seeing, hearing, touching, tasting, and smelling. **Learning** is not something you do only in school. You keep on **learning** throughout your life.

leave "Goodbye. I have to **leave**," you say. When you **leave**, you go away from a place. After you **leave** the party, you have **left**. It is good manners to thank the people who invited you when you **leave** the party.

legs You have two **legs**. Your dog has four **legs**. A centipede has many **legs**. No matter how many there are, **legs** are very useful in getting from here to there. People had **legs** before they had cars.

lemon You need **lemons** if you want to set up a **lemonade** stand. If you bite a **lemon**, it tastes terrible. But if you mix **lemon** juice with water and sugar and ice, it is delicious. Limes are related to **lemons**, but limes are small and green.

200

let "I'll **let** you ride my reindeer," you say. **Let** means allow or give permission. When you **let** your friend ride your reindeer, you give him your permission to do it.

lie There are two words that are spelled **lie**. One word **lie** is what you do in your bed. You **lie** in bed. The other word **lie** means a story or an explanation that is not true. "A dragon ate my mittens," says Greg. Greg knows he left his mittens at his friend's house.

life **Life** is a force or a power you have. A thing that has **life** can take in food, and can grow or change. Anything that does not have **life** is dead. A tree has **life**, but a rock is dead. A thing that has **life** is **alive** or **living**.

201

light When it is completely dark, you bump into things. But if you have **light,** you can see where you are going. **Light** is energy that comes from the sun or a lamp or a flashlight. There is another word **light** which means not heavy. A feather is **light.**

lightning A bright white flash you see during a rainstorm is **lightning.** That **lightning** is a strong bolt of electricity. **Lightning** is powerful stuff that can knock down trees and start forest fires.

like "Judy looks **like** Joan to me," you say. That word **like** means similar to. It's hard to tell the difference between Judy and Joan. There is another word **like** which means that something or someone pleases you. "I **like** orange popsicles." You are pleased and happy when you have an orange popsicle.

lion It's all right to look at a **lion** in a circus or a zoo, but it's a bad idea to keep a **lion** in your home. A **lion** eats a lot of meat, and has a bad habit of roaring. This scares the neighbors.

listen When you **listen,** you give all your attention to what is coming in through your ears. "**Listen** to that wind howl," says your friend. You **listen.**

little "This chair is **little,**" says Tim. If the chair is so small that Tim can't sit on it, it is **little.** A two-foot whale would be **little,** but a two-foot goldfish would be big. It only takes a **little** time to get Tim a bigger chair.

long   Ten blocks is a **long** way to have to carry that heavy bag of groceries. A thing that is **long** has **length.** An eight-foot board is **long,** but a stubby pencil is short. If your birthday is eleven months away, that is a **long** time.

look   **Look** means to do the same thing with your eyes that you do with your ears when you listen. When you **look,** you give all your attention to what is coming in through your eyes. When you want to understand a picture, you **look** at it carefully.

loose   "My tooth is **loose,**" you say. It wobbles and wiggles. Pretty soon it will come out. A thing that is **loose** is not fastened tight. A tiger that is **loose** is not fastened at all. Stay out of the way of that tiger.

lose If you **lose** your dime in the sand, you probably won't ever find it. If you really **lose** something, it's gone forever. Once in a while, you can find what you **lost.**

loud "Wow! That cannon was **loud,**" says Jenny. A thing that is **loud** is a noise of some kind that is so powerful it hurts your ears. Rabbits are seldom **loud.** Firecrackers are almost always **loud.**

love There are lots of people you like, but probably only a few people you **love. Love** is a stronger feeling than like. You like your friend's dog, but you **love** your dog. You get mad at your sister, but you still **love** her.

low Low is down there somewhere. A bush that is only as tall as your knees may look **low** to you, but it may look high to the caterpillar under it. A valley is a **low** place, and a mountain is a high place.

luck If you are walking along and find a dollar on the sidewalk, you arc **lucky. Lucky** is some good thing that happens for no reason at all. The person who lost that dollar is **unlucky.** If you find out who lost that dollar, and you give it back, then he is **lucky.**

lunch "I am having pickles and cake for **lunch,**" says Larry. That is a rather strange **lunch. Lunch** is the meal you eat in the middle of the day.

abcdefghijklmnopqrstuvwxyz

machine Any kind of thing that you use to help you do something or move something is a **machine.** A hammer that you use to pound a nail into a board is a very simple kind of **machine.** An automobile is a more complicated **machine** because it has a lot more parts.

mad Mostly, when they use the word **mad,** people mean angry. "I'm **mad** at him." Sometimes they use **mad about** to say they like something a lot. "I'm **mad about** hot popcorn." Sometimes people say, "He's **mad,**" meaning, "He's crazy." It all sounds confusing, but don't get **mad** about it.

magic "It must have been **magic** that made the dove come out of that sardine can," your friend thinks. She doesn't know the secret of the trick, but you do. The **magic** things you see **magicians** do are just tricks that are meant to fool you. Nobody has ever proved that there is real **magic.**

magnet A **magnet** has an invisible power that pulls some things to it. You have probably seen small **magnets** and know what they can do. A really big **magnet** can lift a whole car. A super big **magnet** could lift a skyscraper.

mail **Mail** is a letter or a magazine or a package that a **mail carrier** brings to your house. "Was there any **mail** for me?" you ask. When you **mail** a letter to a friend, you put it in a **mailbox.** Don't forget the stamp.

make When you **make** a cake, you start with flour and eggs and milk and sugar and a lot more things that don't look like each other. After you mix them together and bake them in an oven, you have **made** a cake. To **make** something is to create something that didn't exist before.

male A **male** is any creature that can become a father. A **male** dog can become a father dog. A **male** fish can become a father to several hundred baby fish at one time. It's a good thing he doesn't have to try to think up names for all of them.

man A boy will grow up to be a **man**. But **man** has many more meanings. **Mankind** means all people—**men,** women, and children of all colors. **Man** is the only creature that can read and talk and write and do other things that you can do.

manners Your **manners** are the ways you do things. If you always remember to say "Please" and "Thank you," people will say you have good **manners**. **Manners** mostly have to do with the way you treat other people.

210

many If you have 16 guinea pigs, you have **many** guinea pigs. Most people only have one or two. **Many** means there are a whole lot of things, maybe so **many** you can't count them all. If you look up at the sky on a clear night, there are so **many** stars you can't count them.

march "I'm going to **march** in the parade tomorrow," you say. When a band or an army **marches,** they all start off together with the same foot and at the same time. They keep in step. **March** is also the name for the month when Spring begins.

marshmallow You can't crack a nut with a **marshmallow.** A **marshmallow** is a very soft puffy candy. **Marshmallows** would make a good pillow, except that your hair would get awfully sticky. Many people like to toast **marshmallows** over a campfire.

mask That weird thing you put on your face at Halloween is a **mask**. A **mask** is meant to hide your face so people can't tell who you are. Some Halloween **masks** are meant to be scary or funny.

match "These socks don't **match**," says Mark. One is green and one is yellow. When things **match**, they look exactly alike. Look for another green sock. There is a different word **match** which means a small stick of some sort with stuff on the end of it that will start a fire.

may "Yes, you **may** go to the snail race," says your mother. **May** means she gives you permission to go. "Take your raincoat. It **may** rain." That means it might rain. The rain won't hurt your snail.

meal A popsicle is not exactly a **meal**. A **meal** is the food you eat at home or in a restaurant for breakfast, lunch, or dinner. Often, you have two or three or more kinds of food at a **meal**.

mean "I know what you **mean**," you say. You understand the words that your friend said. "That frog is **mean**," he said. The frog is nasty and bad-tempered. **Mean** can **mean** a number of different things.

measure When you **measure** something, you find out how long, how high, how deep, how hot, how heavy, or how something else the thing is. Your doctor uses a **measuring** rod to find out how tall you are, and a scale to **measure** how much you weigh.

meat The kinds of food that come from animals are called **meat.** Hamburger, steak, hot dogs, pork chops, ham, and lots of other foods like those are **meat. Meat** is a basic food for most people, but some people never eat **meat.** They call themselves vegetarians. They eat only vegetables.

medicine Anything they give you when you are sick that is supposed to make you get well is **medicine.** It used to be that most **medicine** tasted terrible. Today, most of it is not so bad, but you had better not take any **medicine** unless your doctor or your parents give it to you.

meet "I will **meet** you at four o'clock at the tree where the bluebird is," you say. That means you and your friend will come together at the same place at the same time. "Wilbur, I'd like you to **meet** my friend Walt," says William. When you are introduced to somebody for the first time, you **meet** him.

melt When ice **melts,** it becomes water. A thing that **melts** changes from a solid thing to a liquid that you can pour. A popsicle **melts** on your tongue when you lick it. Even iron will **melt** if you make it hot enough.

memory "I remember the winter when the snow was eight feet deep," you say. That snowstorm is in your **memory.** Your **memory** is all the things that you remember. Your computer has a **memory,** too, but it can only remember the things you tell it.

mend If you know how to **mend** bikes, pants, sailboats, roofs, or other things, you are a pretty good **mender.** When you **mend** something, you fix it. If it is broken or torn or leaky, you make it okay again. It's great if you know how to **mend** things.

merry When you are **merry,** you are happy and laughing and full of good spirits. Kids sometimes get **merry** at a slumber party. They laugh and make a lot of racket. Nobody can get to sleep when everybody is that **merry.**

message A **message** is important information that you send to somebody or to a bunch of somebodies or that is sent to you. A **message** can be sent by phone, by mail, by telegram, by smoke signals, or by a **messenger.** If you are asked to carry a **message** about the cattle rustlers, make sure the **message** gets there in time.

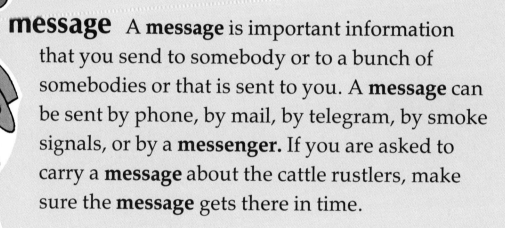

metal Iron, silver, gold, aluminum, and copper are all **metals.** Most **metals** are hard. Most **metals** are whitish, but gold is yellowish and copper is orangish. **Metal** things last a long time, and they don't break as easily as glass or wooden or plastic things do.

216

microscope With a **microscope** you can see all kinds of very tiny creatures that your eyes could not possibly see without help. A **microscope** magnifies things. It makes things seem much bigger than they really are. Put a drop of pond water under a **microscope.** You will see strange animals that you never could see before.

middle If there are three kids in a line, and one of them is in front of you and one of them is in back of you, you are in the **middle. Middle** means about the same as center or in-between.

midget A three-foot-tall man would be called a **midget.** A **midget** is a fully grown thing that is extra small. If you had an elephant that you could hold on your hand, that would be a **midget** elephant.

might The best way to explain **might** is to say maybe. "It looks like it **might** rain," you say. Maybe it will, and maybe it won't. **Might** also means power. "He had the **might** to move mountains." That is pretty **mighty**.

mile "We have only seven more **miles** to go to get to the camp," you say to the campers. That's a pretty long way. A **mile** is 5,280 feet long. You wouldn't have as far to go if it were seven kilometers to the camp. A kilometer is five-eighths of a **mile**.

milk If you like to drink **milk**, that's good, because **milk** has lots of things in it that are good for you. The **milk** you drink comes from cows, but in other parts of the world, people drink **milk** that comes from goats, yaks, and other creatures.

218

mind "To my **mind,** Grace would be the best one to be club president," you say. Your **mind** is your total thinking. Your **mind** includes all that you remember, and all that you have thought about. Except for your body, your **mind** is you.

minute Try to hold your breath for a **minute.** A **minute** is 60 seconds of time. Count in your mind like this, "one-second-one, two-second-two, three-second-three," and so on. When you get to sixty, you will be very close to a **minute.** When you think of it that way, a **minute** seems like a long time.

mirror The face that looks back at you when you look in a **mirror** is a reflection of your face. But everything gets turned around in a **mirror.** The right side of your face becomes the left side in the **mirror.** A **mirror** is a hunk of glass with silver on the back side of it.

mischief Mischief is something we do that we shouldn't do. If you hide your sister's new bicycle, that is **mischief**. **Mischief** causes trouble for other people. It can cause trouble for you when you get caught.

miss "Charlie, you **missed** that pass," says the coach. Charlie didn't catch it. If you shoot an arrow at a target and don't hit the target, you **miss** it. Usually **miss** means you didn't hit it or catch it or something like that. **Miss** can also mean you feel sorry. You **miss** your friend who moved away.

mistake Putting your right shoe on your left foot, and your left shoe on your right foot is a **mistake.** You will feel uncomfortable, and you will have trouble walking. A **mistake** is a wrong thing. Hanging Easter eggs on a Christmas tree would be a **mistake.**

mitten You may have heard a poem about three little kittens who lost their **mittens.** It's not true. Kittens don't wear **mittens.** A **mitten** is a kind of glove that has one hole for your thumb to go into, and a bigger hole for your other four fingers to go into in a bunch.

mix "I'm going to **mix** this blue paint and this yellow paint to make green paint. When you **mix** something, you stir all the things together until you can't tell one thing from another. When you have it all **mixed,** what you now have is a **mixture.**

modern A thing that is **modern** is up-to-date. That means it is a new style, or something that was invented not long ago. A color TV set or VCR would be called **modern,** but an old wind-up phonograph would not.

moment Moment is a strange word. It's sort of slippery. "I'll be there in a **moment,**" says your friend. Nobody knows how long that **moment** will be. It might be ten seconds or ten minutes. Then there is that **moment** when you win the prize for growing the biggest pumpkin. That is a **moment** you will remember.

money If you have **money,** you can buy a new hat. **Money** is pieces of paper and hunks of metal that everybody agrees are worth something. The North American Indians used polished shells as **money.** They called it wampum.

monkey Monkeys always seem to be having lots of fun. **Monkeys** leap around a lot and can hang by their tails. **Monkeys** have hands and faces that make them look quite human. If someone calls you a **monkey,** take it as a compliment. It means the person thinks you are active and full of fun.

monster Monsters are storybook animals. All **monsters** are large, ugly, and strangely built. One Greek **monster,** the Hydra, had many heads. When one head was cut off, two more heads grew in its place. For some reason, kids like to watch **monster** movies, even though they are afraid to look at the screen sometimes.

month If you are going away for a **month's** vacation, don't do it in February. February is the shortest **month** in the year. A **month** is a length of time. Our calendar has 12 **months,** and each **month** has 28, 30, or 31 days. In Leap Year, February has 29 days.

moon We know now for sure that the **moon** is not made of green cheese. The **moon** is made of mountains and rocks and dust. Astronauts have been there and brought back samples of the **moon.** When astronauts walked on the **moon** and looked at the Earth, the Earth looked like a giant blue **moon** to them.

mop A **mop** is used with soap and water to get the dirt that a broom can't sweep up off the floor. You would probably need a **mop** to clean your lion's cage.

more "I'd like some **more** chocolate chip pancakes, please," you say. **More** means you already had one helping, but now you want some extra pancakes. If you have three hats, and a friend gives you two hats, you will have **more** hats than you had before.

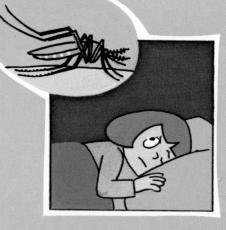

mosquito Nothing is more annoying than the buzz of a **mosquito** when you are in bed at night. You can't see that **mosquito,** but you know it wants to bite you. If it does, you will have a **mosquito** bite — an itchy red bump.

moss That green stuff that grows in damp places in forests and on the trunks of trees is **moss**. **Mosses** are green plants, and most of them are very small. If you look closely at **moss,** you will discover that it is quite pretty.

most If you find the greatest number of eggs at the Easter Egg Hunt, you find the **most.** If you have the **most,** everybody else has fewer eggs. "**Most** of the kids want to go bowling," you say. That means the greatest number of kids want to go bowling.

moth A butterfly flies around in the daytime, but most **moths** prefer to fly in the nighttime. You would have to ask a **moth** why he likes to do that. **Moths** look a lot like butterflies, except that **moths** tend to have heavier bodies.

mother Every **mother** of a child is a woman. Kittens and puppies have **mothers,** but their **mothers** are cats and dogs. A baby turtle has a **mother,** but he never sees her. A **mother** turtle lays her eggs in sand or mud and then goes away.

motor The thing that makes a car or an electric beater go is its **motor.** Some **motors** work on gasoline, and some use electricity. There are wind-up **motors** in some toys, but they don't run very long. Try to invent a **motor** that works on grass. People will call you a hero.

mountain "I don't know if I can climb that **mountain,**" you say. It looks awfully high and steep. A **mountain** is a high place that sticks up from the surface of the land. Some **mountains** are so high they have snow on top of them all year long.

mouse   Your **mouse** has millions of cousins. **Mice** live in almost every part of the world. A **mouse** can't fight very well. So to avoid trouble with enemies, like cats, a **mouse** stays hidden much of the time. That is why you never see many **mice.**

mouth   You know where your **mouth** is. Your **mouth** is the hole near the bottom of your face where the food goes in, and the words come out. Every animal has to have a **mouth** of some kind so it can eat. A shark has a big **mouth** with a lot of sharp teeth. Sharks don't talk.

move   Raise your hand. You just **moved** your hand. Whenever you change something from one place to another, you **move** it. A horse that is running is **moving.** He is not standing in the same spot.

much "He has **much** money," Irene says. **Much** means a lot of, or a great amount of. "Who shall we invite to the party?" asks your friend. "I haven't thought **much** about it." That means you haven't spent a lot of time thinking about it.

mud When it rains, all the dirt turns to **mud. Mud** is nothing but dirt and water. There are different kinds of **mud,** depending on the dirt. Some kinds of **mud** are sticky, and some kinds of **mud** are slippery. Most people don't care much for **mud,** so don't take it in the house.

mule A **mule** is a strange animal that is part horse and part jackass. A **mule** is big, strong, and usually stubborn. Sometimes getting a **mule** to move is about as easy as getting water to run uphill. **Mules** were often used for pulling wagons in the West.

muscle Muscle is the softish part of your arms or your legs that is between the skin and the bones. **Muscles** are a bit like rubber bands. They can stretch out or pull back. **Muscles** are fastened to your bones, and they can make your bones move.

music Sounds that make a pattern or that join together in a pleasing way are called **music.** A kid playing on a guitar can make **music.** An orchestra can make **music.** A singer or a group of singers can make **music.** A bunch of people honking automobile horns in a traffic jam make nothing but noise.

must "I **must** get these tomatoes picked before the snow comes," you say. A **must** thing is a thing you have to do. You **must** get a glass before you pour the milk, or the milk will go on the floor.

mustard Mustard is the yellow, spicy stuff that goes on hot dogs and hamburgers. The **mustard** you eat is made from the small seeds of a **mustard** plant. These **mustard** seeds are ground up and mixed with a liquid like water or vinegar.

mystery If nobody can understand how the chicken got into the closet, that is a **mystery.** A **mystery** is something that nobody understands or can explain. How that chicken got into the closet is very **mysterious.**

myth A **myth** is a story that has been believed by a people for a long time, maybe for hundreds of years. The Greeks had **myths** about their gods and ancient heroes. The North American Indians have **myths** about their gods and long-ago heroes.

abcdefghijklmnopqrstuvwxyz

name You know what your **name** is. When you meet a new kid in the neighborhood, you ask, "What is your **name?**" A **name** is a special word we give to a person or a thing so that everybody will know who or what we mean when we use that **name.** Be proud of your own **name.**

nap A short sleep in the afternoon is called a **nap.** Sometimes you fall asleep in a car without meaning to. That sleep would be called a **nap.** When your cat curls up on the rug for a sleep, that is called a **cat nap.**

near When you are **near** the ocean, you can hear the waves and smell the sea air. **Near** means close to. If a friend lives **near** you, he lives not far away. There are some things it is good not to be **near** to. It is not a good idea to live **near** a boiler factory. The noise is terrible.

neck The part of you between your chin and your shoulders is your **neck.** Your **neck** connects your head with the rest of you. A snake seems to be mostly all **neck,** but that is not really true. The champion **neck** grower is the giraffe.

need "We're going to **need** lots of water to make it across that desert," you say. There is no place to get water on the desert so you have to take the water you will **need** with you. When you **need** something, you have to have it. You **need** water to stay alive in a desert.

neighbor, neighbour ✿

Someone who lives near you is your **neighbor.** You are a **neighbor** to that person. The part of town where you live is your **neighborhood.** Any **neighborhood** is a good place to live if all the **neighbors** are friendly to each other.

233

never "I'm **never** going in there again," you say. "It's too scary." **Never** is a strong word. It means not again, not now, not ever. Be careful when you use **never.** "I **never** want to see you again," says your friend. Maybe next week your friend wants to see you again.

new If your radio breaks, you may have to buy a **new** one. That means it just came from the factory. No one ever used it before. Things that just happened are **news.** You can listen to the **news** on your **new** radio.

next "You're **next,**" says the ice cream man. "What flavor do you want?" **Next** means it's your turn right after the person who was in front of you. Make up your mind what flavor you want, because now the person who is behind you is **next.**

nice There are some words that don't really have any meaning that can be explained. **Nice** is one of those words. **Nice** just means you like it. "It's a **nice** day." The sun is shining, and you feel good. **Nice** people are people you like. They probably think you are **nice,** too.

nickel "How far can I travel for a **nickel?**" you ask the taxi driver. "Not very far," he says. A **nickel** is a coin that buys the same amount that five pennies will buy. If you can buy one pretzel for one penny, you can buy five pretzels for a **nickel.**

night You don't get to see much of the **night,** because you are asleep through most of it. **Night** is the time when your part of the world is dark. **Night** is a quiet time because most people are in bed. But when it is **night** where you are, it is day on the other side of the world.

235

nine With **nine** apples, you can make a lot of applesauce. But peeling and cooking **nine** apples is some job. **Nine** is one more than eight. You will get more applesauce from **nine** apples than you would from eight. The numeral that stands for **nine** is 9.

no **No** is a word to tell you that you can't do it, or you can't have it, or that something is not so. A **No** Parking sign means you can't park at that place. If everybody says **no** all the time, nothing gets done.

noise A loud sound, or a lot of ugly sounds mixed together, is **noise**. Cars honking and bus motors roaring on a city street are **noise**. A bunch of kids yelling and making happy sounds on a playground may sound like **noise** to some people, but not to others.

none   If you are completely out of weasels, you have **none.** If you have **none,** that means you don't even have one. The next time, remember to close the door of your weasel cage. Instead of **none,** then you will still have some.

north   "**North** is that way," says the Eskimo. He is pointing toward the **North** Pole. When you go **north,** usually the weather gets colder and colder. When you get close to the **North** Pole, you need heavy socks and earmuffs.

nose   Your **nose** always goes in front of you. Your **nose** sticks out from the middle of your face. Your **nose** is the thing that you breathe with and that you smell with. "Follow your **nose**" is an old expression. Ask your favorite bloodhound what it means. He knows.

nothing "There is **nothing** to eat in the cupboard," you say. **Nothing** is made from the words no and thing. There is no thing in the cupboard for you to eat. When there is **nothing** to eat, you get pretty hungry.

now "Let's go to the movie **now**," says your friend. **Now** means right this minute, not later. If you don't go to the movie **now**, you might miss the cartoon.

number "How many hamburgers can you eat?" asks your friend. "Three," you say. Three is a **number**. It is a **number** that tells your friend how many hamburgers you can eat. A **number** always tells how many or how much.

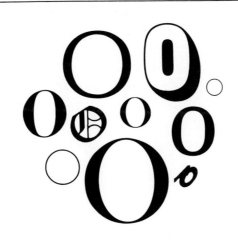

abcdefghijklmnopqrstuvwxyz

oar   You need **oars** if you hope to make a rowboat go anyplace. And you have to move those **oars** very fast if you hope to catch that seal. **Oars** are large paddles you can use to make a boat go if you don't have a motor or a sail.

ocean   A porpoise could tell you that most of our world is covered with **oceans.** An **ocean** is a giant hunk of water that is hundreds or thousands of miles wide. North America has the Atlantic **Ocean** on one side of it and the Pacific **Ocean** on the other side.

octopus   It's hard to believe that an **octopus** is real. An **octopus** is a sea creature that has a head, a body, and eight arms. That's all. If an **octopus** ever has to scratch himself, he has plenty of arms to do it with.

odd "That's **odd**," you say. "I've never seen it snow in July before." An **odd** thing is something that is unusual or peculiar. You don't expect it. **Odd** also means any number you can't divide into two equal parts. Five is an **odd** number. If you have five oranges, you can't share them equally with your brother unless you cut one of the oranges.

of "My new shirt is made **of** grass," says Otto. He means the person who made the shirt used grass to make it. **Of** is a little word that hooks other words together. **Of** really gets its meaning from the other words around it. It is very hard to think **of** all **of** the ways to use **of**.

off **Off** is not much easier to think about than **of**. You get **off** a pony or a bus. A star is a long way **off**. **Off** usually has to do with distance or time, but it can also mean no longer working. You turn your record player **off**.

okay Okay is a simple word that means you like or think well of something. "That movie is **okay.**" You liked it. If you think a new kid who moved next door is **okay,** that means you like him or her.

old "That's really an **old** car," you say. **Old** can mean a very long time ago, or it can mean not so long ago. "I'm five years **old,**" your friend says. That's how long it's been since your friend was born. Five years is not really very **old.**

on When you put your hat **on,** you put it **on** your head. It stays there unless the wind blows it off. If you have figured out what off means, you won't have any trouble with **on.** **On** means the opposite of off. If you want to play a record, you turn your record player **on.**

once "I tasted rhubarb **once,** and I didn't like it," you tell Tillie. Usually **once** means only one time. "I feed my shark **once** a day," you say. That means you feed your shark only one time each day.

one You have to understand what **one** means before you can understand two or three or all the other numbers. You are **one** person. You have **one** head and **one** nose. When you point, you point with **one** finger.

only If you have the **only** green robin in the world, that means nobody else has a green robin. **Only** usually means one of a kind. "I'm the **only** person in the neighborhood who can wiggle his ears," you say. Nobody else can do it.

open Turn a doorknob and pull. The door is now **open.** The door is not closed now, and you can go in or out. When you **open** a bag of peanuts, you can take peanuts out or put peanuts back in.

opportunity "You can have this genuine pirate map," says the man. If the map is real, you have an **opportunity** to find buried treasure. An **opportunity** is a chance to make something good happen. If you see somebody in trouble, you have an **opportunity** to help.

or You are either asleep **or** awake. You can't be both at the same time. "You can have chocolate **or** vanilla **or** strawberry ice cream for dessert," says the waiter. **Or** means you have to pick one. You can't have them all.

orange   If the **oranges** on your **orange** tree look green, don't pick them yet. When an **orange** is ripe, it has an **orangish** color. If you want to make the color **orange** with paints, mix yellow and red together.

ordinary   The clothes you wear almost every day are your **ordinary** clothes. Your **ordinary** clothes are different from the fancy clothes you wear for special times. **Ordinary** food is the kind of food you eat almost every day, not the special feast you eat on Thanksgiving.

other   "I don't like that red bicycle. I'd rather have the **other** one," you say. **Other** usually means something else. "My **other** pants are dirty, so I had to wear my green ones."

ouch When you fall down and bang your knee on a rock, you say, "**Ouch!**" Ouch is a word that everybody seems to understand. You only say **ouch** when something hurts. Put a bandage on that cut knee.

ought "I **ought** to put that fish back in his bowl and clean up the water," you say. **Ought** means you should do it. The cat knocked the bowl over, but it's up to you to take care of things. The fish needs to be put back in his bowl, and that water **ought** to be cleaned up.

our "You can't come in **our** clubhouse unless you join **our** club," you say. When you say **our,** it means a thing doesn't belong just to you, but to you and other people, too. "That's **our** windmill." The windmill belongs to you and your whole family.

out If you go **out** of your house, you leave your house, and you go **outside.** If you go **out** of your bedroom and go into the kitchen, you are still in the house. When you are in the kitchen, you might find **out** you are **out** of bananas. There are no bananas. **Out** is a strange kind of word.

over When you say, "That blimp is **over** my head," you mean it is above you. It is higher than you. If you go into water that is **over** your head, that means when you stand on the bottom, the top of the water is above your head. **Over** can also mean again. "You goofed when you played that last song," the music teacher says. "Play it **over.**"

owe "Here's the dime I **owe** you," says your friend. He borrowed the dime from you to buy a bicycle. If you borrow something from somebody, you owe it. You have to give it back. "Here's the owl I **owe** you," you say.

247

owl You probably don't get to see an **owl** very often. An **owl** is a largish bird that flies around at night and hides somewhere during the day. **Owls** have large eyes that help them see in the dark. **Owls** have a reputation for being wise. They really don't deserve it.

own "I **own** this desert," you say. When you **own** something, it belongs to you. When you **own** anything, you are the **owner** of that thing. It's your problem to figure out what to do with that desert you **own.**

oyster If you like a quiet pet, get an **oyster.** An **oyster** never makes any noise. An **oyster** always stays in one place. There are a couple of things wrong with having an **oyster** for a pet. You will probably never get to see him because he lives between two hard shells. And you need an ocean to keep him in.

abcdefghijklmno**pq**rstuvwxyz

package "I wonder what's in that **package**," you say. A **package** is a wrapped thing, or a box with something in it. Maybe an ant farm or 12 jars of peanut butter or 16 pairs of sneakers are in that **package.** You have to open the **package** to find out.

page You are looking at a **page**. A **page** is one side of a sheet of paper in a book. A sheet of paper in a book is called a leaf. That kind of leaf is not the same kind of leaf that falls off a tree. Just read this **page** and then go on to the next **page.**

paint Paint is colored stuff people put on walls, wagons, doors, floors, and other things. It is a bad idea to put **paint** on windows, because then you can't see out. A picture made with **paint** on paper or canvas is called a **painting.** The person who did it is a **painter.**

250

pair Two red shoes that match each other are a **pair.** One red shoe and one boot are not a **pair,** because **pair** means two things that are alike. Twins are called a **pair.**

pajamas Most people would think it strange if you wore your **pajamas** to the supermarket. Usually people wear **pajamas** when they go to bed. Our word **pajamas** comes from Persia, where **pajamas** were invented.

pan If you plan to eat beans on your camping trip, remember to take a **pan** to cook them in. If you plan to eat bacon, take a frying **pan.** If you have to cook soup for 50 people, you should have a pot. A pot is bigger and deeper than a **pan.**

pancake Syrup tastes better on **pancakes** than mustard does. **Pancakes** are round, flat things made of dough and cooked in a frying pan. **Pancakes** are great for breakfast, especially when you're hungry.

pants "My **pants** are too long," says Pam. **Pants** are just one thing, but we say pair of **pants,** as if **pants** were two. **Pants** cover your two legs. That is why we say pair of **pants.** When your dog **pants,** that's something different. He's breathing short and fast. He's not wearing **pants.**

paper You don't have to write on a rock when you want to send a message to a friend. You have **paper. Paper** is great stuff. Think of all the ways you use **paper. Paper** is made from trees. You are looking at **paper** now.

parachute "I'm glad my **parachute** opened," you say. A **parachute** is a very large hunk of cloth that lets you float down gently if you jump out of an airplane. If you decide not to jump out of the airplane, you don't need your **parachute.**

parade If you march your snake in the pet **parade,** tell him to keep his head up and to keep in step. A **parade** is a bunch of people marching together or moving together to celebrate some event. Some people would rather be in a **parade,** and some would rather watch a **parade.**

parent If you wonder what a **parent** is, ask a mother or father. That's who a **parent** is, a mother or a father. Some **parents,** like fish and spiders, don't take care of their offspring, but most **parents** do.

253

park "I think I'll take my panda to the **park,**" you say. Your panda will probably have fun in the **park.** A **park** has grass and trees, places to play games, and other things to do. When your father or mother **parks** the car, that's a different kind of **park.** That kind of **park** means to put something in a special place.

parrot Conversations with a **parrot** are usually pretty dull. **Parrots** don't really talk. They just repeat words or sounds people have taught them. After you hear a **parrot** say, "Awk, I'm a pretty bird," 30 times, you probably wish the **parrot** would shut up.

part "I put that clock back together, but I have this **part** left over," you say. A **part** is a piece of something. The clock probably won't work without that **part.** You may have to take the clock **apart** again and find out where that **part** belongs.

party   At a rabbit **party,** rabbits eat
a lot of carrots and do dances like
the bunny hop. At a monkey **party,**
they eat bananas and leap around
a lot. At a people **party,** you and
your friends eat and drink the
things you like, and play games
or do other things you like to do.

paste   **Paste** is stuff you use to make
one piece of paper stick to another
piece of paper. You also use **paste** when
you want to **paste** wallpaper on a wall.
Make sure you don't **paste** that wallpaper
across the door. It will be hard to find
out how to get out of the room.

path   "I wonder if this **path** leads
to the waterfall," you say.
A **path** is a sort of clear trail
where other people have walked
before. You can't always be
sure where a **path** will lead you.
Try it and find out.

paw Ask your dog about **paws.** He knows about **paws** because he has four of them. An animal's **paw** is a bit like a hand or a foot on a human. A **paw** has things like toes, and things like nails or claws. No animal's **paw** can do the things your hands can do.

pea Blue **peas** and square **peas** don't exist. Most **peas** are green and round. **Peas** are seeds of the **pea** plant, and when they are picked fresh, they are delicious. Sometimes it's a little hard to chase **peas** around on your plate with your fork, because the **peas** roll around.

peace When you and your brother or sister or friend are having fun together, and doing things together, and helping each other, you have **peace.** When nations enjoy each other and help each other, there is **peace.** When they fight each other, there is war. **Peace** is more healthy and enjoyable than war.

peach "This **peach** feels hairy," says Harry. That **peach** is not really hairy; it just has a kind of fuzz on its skin. A **peach** is a sweet, juicy, yellowish fruit almost everyone likes. Inside a **peach** is one large seed. If you plant that seed, it will grow to be a **peach** tree.

peanut Tell your favorite elephant not to look up in a tree for **peanuts,** because **peanuts** grow under the ground. An elephant can't dig up **peanuts** unless you lend him a shovel.

pear A **pear** is a fruit with a strange shape, because it is bigger at the bottom than at the top. A **pear** tastes the same all over, so it really doesn't matter. If you have two **pears,** you have a pair of **pears.**

pencil "I have to sharpen my **pencil**," you say. A **pencil** is a long, skinny piece of wood with some stuff called graphite inside. This graphite makes black marks on paper and other things. It's the graphite that makes a **pencil** a **pencil**. There are **pencils** that make marks in colors. These have colored stuff instead of graphite inside.

people Creatures walking around on two legs are **people,** unless they are bears. It is usually fairly easy to tell which are **people**. **People** means humans. You are a human. One human is a person. A bunch of persons are **people**.

perfect "That's a **perfect** pie," Pat says. A thing that is **perfect** is the greatest. It couldn't be any better. It's hard to be **perfect** about everything you do, but don't let that stop you from trying.

perhaps If you get tired of saying maybe, you can surprise people by saying **perhaps. Perhaps** means the same thing as maybe. "**Perhaps** that fish will bite the bait," you say. Maybe it will, and maybe it won't.

permanent "That mountain looks **permanent** to me," you say. **Permanent** means it's going to be there tomorrow and next year and for a long, long time to come. A snowflake is not **permanent.** It disappears when spring comes.

permission If you ask your parents to let you go to Africa to hunt penguins, you ask for their **permission.** If they give you their **permission,** they **permit** you to go. It's not very likely they will give their **permission.** Penguins do not live in Africa. They live near the South Pole.

pet Some towns have **pet** shows every year. People bring their **pets** to show them off. There are **pet** snakes, rabbits, lizards, fish, cats, turtles, raccoons, birds, and other creatures. If you show your **pet** flea, people will have trouble seeing your **pet.**

phonograph Phonograph is a long word that means record player. The **phone** part of the word comes from an old Greek word that means sound. The **graph** part comes from a Greek word that means write. A **phonograph** record has sound written on it in a special way. When you play the **phonograph** record, you can hear the sounds.

photograph You use a camera when you want to take a **photograph** of your cat jumping over the fence. **Photograph** comes from Greek words that mean light and write. It's easier to take a **photograph** of your cat jumping over the fence than it is to paint a picture of it.

piano "I'm sorry, but I left my **piano** at home. Can I borrow yours?" you ask. A **piano** can make great music if you know how to play it. But a **piano** is too big and heavy to carry around. Have you tried playing the harmonica?

pick "Take your **pick.** You can have any piece of candy you want," says Edith. You can **pick,** or choose, one piece from the box. When you go to a field to **pick** strawberries, you **pick** all the ones that are red and ripe.

picture A **picture** is a drawing or photograph of something. You could draw a **picture** of your favorite pork chop, or you could use a camera to take a **picture** of it. Whichever way you do it, people could look at your **picture** and say, "Wow, that's a great pork chop!"

pie   Nearly all the **pies** you see are round. Once in a while somebody decides to be different and makes a square **pie. Pies** have a crust on the bottom and something else on top, like apples, custard, tomatoes, or peaches. Four and twenty blackbirds baked in a **pie** is not a good idea, in spite of what the nursery rhyme says.

piece   "I'd like another **piece** of whole wheat bread, please," you say. A **piece** is just a part or a hunk of something. You don't want a whole loaf of bread. You just want a **piece** of it. Try toasting that **piece** of bread and then put butter and honey on it.

pig   Be kind to your **pig. Pigs** are smart animals. They were one of the very first animals to be trained to live with people. **Pigs** eat a lot, and that is why people who eat a lot are sometimes called **pigs.** That may be an insult to a real **pig.**

pigeon "Take this message to Mary quick," you tell your **pigeon.** Some **pigeons,** called homing **pigeons,** are trained to fly to a certain place. Other **pigeons** just seem to wander all over the place. It is safe to give a secret message to a **pigeon. Pigeons** can't talk.

pillow A brick is not a very good **pillow.** A **pillow** is a thing you rest your head on when you go to bed. Most people prefer a **pillow** that is soft and comfortable. There are large **pillows** people put on the floor and sit on.

pin You know right away when a **pin** is sticking in you. That hurts. A **pin** is a long, thin metal thing with a sharp point. **Pins** are used sometimes to hold clothes together. Then there are bowling **pins,** but they are a different kind of **pin** altogether.

pine "I think a **pine** tree would look good over there," says your father. A **pine** is a kind of tree with long, thin leaves called needles. These needles stay on the tree all year long. **Pine** trees are often used as Christmas trees.

pioneer If you are one of the first persons to move into a wild, unsettled place, you are a **pioneer**. Being a **pioneer** is a lot of hard work. You have to chop down trees to build a house, and you have to lift a lot of heavy rocks. There is no supermarket nearby, so you have to grow or find your own food.

place "This is a great **place**," you say. A **place** where you can get free popcorn, free lemonade, and free hot dogs is a great **place**. A **place** is a particular location. A **place** can be a town, a field, a home, a room, or even a chair. "This is your **place**," says your friend. He is showing you where you are to sit at the party.

plain A **plain** doughnut doesn't have any jelly in it. **Plain** hamburger is just hamburger with nothing on it. **Plain** water is water that doesn't have sugar or flavoring in it. **Plain** is a very **plain** word.

plan "I have a **plan**," you say. You thought of a way to win the snowball battle. A **plan** is something you think out before you do it. A **plan** for a house shows where all the rooms will be. The builder follows that **plan** when he builds the house.

planet You already should have some idea about **planets,** because you are living on one. The **planet** you live on is named Earth. A **planet** is round, and a **planet** travels around a sun. There are eight other **planets** that travel around our sun.

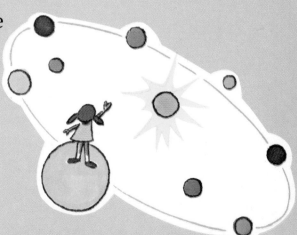

plant If it's green and alive and stays in one place all the time, it has to be a **plant**. A green lamppost is not a **plant** because it is not alive. A few **plants,** like mushrooms, are not green. Some **plants** live in water and float around, but they don't move by themselves.

plastic "This **plastic** apple is hard to chew," you say. Lots of things that look like real wood, or real fruit, or real flowers are made of **plastic. Plastic** is stuff that is made in factories from chemicals. **Plastic** things may look real, but a **plastic** apple will never taste like a real apple that grew on a real tree.

plate Don't put more spaghetti on your **plate** than you are sure you can eat. A **plate** is a flattish dish you eat food from. A **plate** is bigger around and not as deep as a bowl. If you put too much spaghetti on your **plate** and try to eat it all, you won't have room for dessert.

play Lots of people think **play** is doing what you like to do, and that work is doing what you have to do. If you enjoy **playing** the guitar, it is **play** for you. If you don't enjoy **playing** the guitar, then it is work.

pleasant A sunny summer day when you are swimming with friends and having fun is a **pleasant** day. A person who smiles at you, and talks with you, and makes you feel good is a **pleasant** person. A thing that is **pleasant** is something or someone who makes you happy.

please It will **please** your friend if you let him borrow your roller skates. When you **please** somebody, you do something nice that makes that person feel good. **Please** is also a polite word a person uses when he asks for something. ''**Please** bring my skates back when the roller skate race is over,'' you say.

plenty "I have **plenty** of plums," you say. "Have some." A big basket of plums is enough for you, and enough to share with others. **Plenty** means all you need, and maybe even more than you need.

pocket It is not a good idea to put a popsicle in your **pocket**. The popsicle will melt and make your **pocket** soggy and sticky. A **pocket** is a cloth bag sewed into your shirt or skirt or pants. It is okay to put peanuts in your **pocket** but not popsicles. Peanuts don't melt.

point "See if you can hit that **point** on the target," you say. "It's not polite to **point**," your friend says. A **point** is a particular spot or location. **Point** also means what you do with your finger when you aim at something.

police officer A person with a blue uniform and a badge is probably a **police officer. Police officers** actually spend more time helping people who are in trouble than they do catching crooks and robbers. If you are ever in trouble, call a **police officer.**

polish "I have to **polish** this old teakettle," you say. When you **polish** something, you get all the dirt off it, and then you rub it until it shines. You use shoe **polish** when you **polish** your shoes. Be careful not to **polish** your socks when you **polish** your shoes.

polite It's very easy to be **polite.** If you smile and say, "Good morning," to a friend, and she smiles back and says, "Good morning," that makes you feel good. You think she is **polite,** and she thinks you are **polite.**

pond If you want to give your frog a treat, take it to a **pond.** A **pond** is a smallish hunk of water that has land all around it. A **pond** is smaller than a lake. Frogs love **ponds.** When your frog gets into the **pond,** it may not want to come out.

pony Don't expect your **pony** to pull that heavy sleigh. A **pony** is a small horse that is as big as he will ever be. Sometimes people call a young horse that isn't full grown a **pony.** You need some big horses to pull that sleigh.

pool "Last one in the **pool** is a rotten egg," you call. Most people, when they hear the word **pool,** think of a swimming **pool.** There is also a small, shallow **pool** you see in a garden or park. There is a game called **pool,** which is played on a **pool** table.

popcorn Nobody knows who discovered how to make **popcorn**. Maybe it was an accident. Who would think that a small kernel of corn would explode and become a big, white, fluffy piece of **popcorn?** Your **popcorn** will taste better if you put butter and salt on it.

possible "It's **possible** that I can jump across the river," you say. A thing that is **possible** could happen, but that doesn't mean it will happen. If you really believe it is **possible** for you to jump across the river, maybe you can do it if you try hard enough.

potato A **potato** has no use for eyes because it grows under the ground. Actually, the eyes of a **potato** are not used to see with. If you cut them out and plant them, they grow to be new **potato** plants. A **potato** tastes delicious when you boil it, bake it, fry it, or mash it.

power A railroad locomotive has a lot of **power,** but your mouse doesn't have much **power.** **Power** is the ability to do things or to move things. A locomotive has the **power** to pull many big boxcars. A mouse only has **power** enough to pull a small stick.

practice If you **practice** pitching horseshoes or knitting every day, you can get to be very good at either one. When you **practice,** you work at something, and you try to get better and better. If you **practice** knitting long enough, maybe you can knit a sweater for your zebra.

praise "You did a great job of building that birdhouse," says your father. When somebody tells you you did a good job, that is **praise.**

prefer "I **prefer** apricots, thank you," you say. A thing you **prefer** is a thing you like better than other things. You like apricots more than you like turnips or onions. Try peaches. You may discover you **prefer** them.

prepare When it's your turn to fix dinner for the family, you **prepare** the dinner. **Prepare** means you get everything ready. When you **prepare** for a camping trip, you get your sleeping bag, tent, flashlight, and other things ready before you start out.

present **Present** is a wacky word that can confuse you. A **present** is a gift somebody gives you. When you are at a meeting or a party, you are **present.** That means you are there. The **present** also means right now.

pretend If you put a bunch of chairs in a line and sit on the front one and say, "Toot, toot," you **pretend** you are driving a train. **Pretend** means make-believe. See if you can fool your friends by **pretending** to be a fish.

price "The **price** for this statue of a grasshopper is eight dollars," says the man. That is how much you have to pay if you want to buy it. That's a high **price** for a statue of a grasshopper. Ask the man the **price** of a real grasshopper.

MY BEDROOM! KEEP OUT! PRIVATE PROPERTY!

private Your house or apartment is **private**. Nobody can come in unless he is invited. Your bedroom is your **private** room. Your clothes and toys and books are your **private** property. They belong to you.

274

prize A **prize** is something you win because you did something well or because you were just lucky. You win a **prize** if the judges say you made the best fudge.

promise If you **promise** your friend that you will help him paint the shed, you have to do it. A **promise** is something you say you will do. If you don't keep your **promise,** your friend will never believe you again. Help him paint the shed.

prompt "You are very **prompt,**" says the bandleader. **Prompt** means you got there at the time you were supposed to be there. People like it when they can count on you to be **prompt.** The only trouble is you forgot to bring your drum.

275

proper It's **proper** to use your roller skates on the sidewalk, but it's **improper** to use them in your living room. A thing that is **proper** is a thing most people agree is the right thing to do. If you roller skate in the living room, you might skate on the cat's tail. The cat will object.

protect A dragon is a great thing to **protect** your house from burglars. Chain him out front and tell him to breathe fire if a burglar comes near. That will be pretty good **protection.** When you **protect** something, you guard it and keep it safe.

proud "I'm **proud** of my chicken," you say. Your chicken laid 14 eggs in five minutes and won the egg-laying contest. Your chicken probably feels **proud** of herself for having done so well. But your chicken is probably tired after all that work. Take her home to rest.

prove If your friend wants to **prove** that the bone he found is a genuine dinosaur bone, he has to have proof. If two dinosaur experts say it is a dinosaur bone, that probably **proves** he is right. When you **prove** something, you make clear that it is true.

puddle Kids seem to love **puddles.** A **puddle** is a small patch of water that is left after a rainstorm or after snow melts. If you really do want to stomp in that **puddle,** don't do it with your good shoes. Wear boots.

pull "It's hard to **pull** this donkey," Donald says. When you **pull** something, you are in front of it, and you try to make it move toward you. Maybe, instead of **pulling,** you should offer the donkey an apple. Then, maybe, you won't need to **pull.**

pumpkin It's not normal for a **pumpkin** to turn into a carriage. That only happens in fairy stories. A **pumpkin** is a large, roundish, orange fruit. **Pumpkins** are used to make pies, and they are used as jack-o'-lanterns on Halloween.

puppet **Puppets** don't really say all those funny things, even though they seem to. **Puppets** are not alive. They are made of wood and cloth and plastic and other stuff. The person who makes the **puppet** work and who does the talking is a **puppeteer**.

puppy Your **puppy** may look small now, but watch out! It may grow up to be a very big dog. **Puppies** are friendly and likeable animals and do a great deal of tail wagging. You can teach a **puppy** many things, but you cannot teach him to play checkers very well.

278

purpose When you do something on **purpose,** it's a thing you want to do. If you cook ten hot dogs for your friend's birthday party, you do it for the **purpose** of making the guests happy. If you knock over the lemonade pitcher by accident, you didn't do that on **purpose.**

push "Please help me **push** this wagon across the creek," you say. When you **push** something, you get behind it and use your force to try to make it go forward. When you want to ring somebody's doorbell, you **push** the button outside the door.

put **Put** those logs over by the fireplace. When you **put** something somewhere, you set it in a certain place. You **put** your hat on your head. When you come back home, you **put** your hat in the closet.

279

puzzle A **puzzle** is a thing that is hard to figure out. **Puzzles** are made to **puzzle** you. There are maze **puzzles**, jigsaw **puzzles**, and crossword **puzzles**. If you can't figure out how to get those rings apart, you are **puzzled**.

quack Ducks can't say very much. "**Quack**," is all they can manage to say. It seems hard to carry on a conversation when all you can say is "**Quack**." However, ducks say **quack** to each other over and over. Maybe ducks know more about what **quack** means than we do.

quarter If you cut a cake into four equal pieces, each piece is a **quarter** of the cake. A **quarter** is also a coin. If you have four **quarters**, they will buy as much as one dollar, because four **quarters** are the same amount of money as one dollar.

queer "It's **queer** that your dog likes to climb trees," says Kate. A thing that is **queer** is odd or unusual. It is unusual for a dog to want to climb trees. Maybe he likes to sit on bird nests. That's **queer,** too.

question A **question** is something somebody says to you or writes to you that asks for an answer. "How old are you?" someone asks. "One hundred and three," you answer if that is how old you are. If you are that old, you ought to know the answer to a lot of **questions.**

quick If you can get out of bed, wash your face, brush your teeth, get dressed, and get to the breakfast table in five minutes, you are **quick.** A person who is **quick** is able to get things done fast.

quiet When it's **quiet,** there is no noise. A forest is usually a **quiet** place. If you want to sneak up to a rabbit, you move **quietly,** on tiptoe. Rabbits are **quiet** animals, and they can hear almost any noise.

quit When you say, "I'm going to **quit** this dumb game," you stop playing it and you leave. You **quit** because you think it's not a good idea to play soccer with a cannonball. It hurts your foot when you kick it.

quite "The pie isn't **quite** done," your friend says. That means it isn't completely baked yet and will have to stay in the oven a little longer. "Maybe the oven isn't **quite** hot enough," you say. It isn't as hot as it should be.

282

abcdefghijklmnopqrstuvwxyz

rabbit Nobody knows for sure how the idea got started that **rabbits** deliver eggs at Easter. No **rabbit** ever laid an egg. **Rabbits** are smallish animals with large ears and big hind legs. **Rabbits** can run like crazy. You can call a **rabbit** a bunny if you wish.

raccoon A **raccoon** looks like a thief, and some say he acts like a thief. A **raccoon** has what looks like a black mask across his face. **Raccoons** will eat almost anything, and they will even go into garbage cans.

race "I hope I win the one-legged **race**," you say. If you get to the finish line first, you win the **race.** There is another word **race** that means group. You are a member of the human **race,** which is different from any of the other **races** of animals.

radio There are not tiny people inside a **radio** doing all that talking and singing. A **radio** is a marvelous invention that can grab invisible waves out of the air and turn them into sounds you can hear. The people who are doing all that talking and singing are miles away in a **radio** station.

rain Nobody has to tell you what **rain** is, unless you live in a desert. **Rain** is water that falls out of the sky. The next time it **rains,** look up. There has to be a cloud up there, because that's where the **rain** comes from. Wear your **raincoat.**

raisin **Raisins** are wrinkled. A **raisin** is a grape that has been dried in the sun or in an oven. **Raisins** contain iron, which is supposed to be good for you. **Raisins** will not make you rusty.

285

raspberry There are two kinds of **raspberries,** red ones and black ones. Both kinds are delicious. There is a curious thing about the black **raspberry,** however. When it is red, it is still green. That meaning of green means the berry is not ripe yet.

rat It is not an easy life to be a **rat. Rats** hang around garbage cans and places like that. People don't like **rats.** Cats chase them. A **rat** looks like a mouse, except that a **rat** is much bigger.

raw Food that is not cooked is **raw.** Most people think lettuce and carrots taste better **raw.** Meats and potatoes taste better after they are cooked. A cold, chilly wind that makes you shiver is called a **raw** wind. Cook that wind.

reach "I can't **reach** those grapes," says the fox. He has his paw out as far as it will go, but it's not out far enough to grab the grapes. If you **reach** up and get the grapes for the fox, he will probably be very thankful.

read If you can **read,** you can learn almost anything you want to learn. When you **read,** you take in words through your eyes. Blind people **read** specially made books with their fingers. When you **read,** you can learn what people thought and felt and did yesterday or thousands of years ago.

ready "I'm **ready** to go kite flying," you say. You have your kite and string and a tail for the kite. You're **ready.** Now you just have to hope the wind is **ready** to blow your kite up into the sky.

real "Is that a **real** diamond?" your friend asks. A thing that is **real** is truly what it appears to be. A **real** diamond is a diamond, not a piece of glass that has been made to look like a diamond. Fifty cents is a cheap price for a **real** diamond. That diamond is probably false.

recipe If you want to make vanilla fudge stew, you need a **recipe.** A **recipe** tells you how much of each thing you need, how to mix the things together, and how to cook it. Vanilla fudge stew sounds terrible. Maybe you should look for another **recipe.**

recognize "I **recognize** that face," you say. When you **recognize** something, you remember having seen or smelled or heard or touched or tasted it before. You **recognize** the taste of peppermint candy because you tasted it before.

record "I'd like to hear that **record** again," says Ralph. He is talking about that flat, round thing with a hole in the middle. There are also written **records**. "The temperature was 105 today," you write in your diary. You can read that **record** years from now.

red A fire engine is **red,** and so is the stoplight of a car. For some reason, people have agreed that **red** is a danger signal. A **red** flag or a **red** flare on a highway means danger. **Red** is just a color, as blue and yellow are. Enjoy **red.**

refrigerator Things like milk and ice cream that need to be kept cold go into the **refrigerator.** A **refrigerator** is a machine that keeps things cool or frozen. A **refrigerator** can even turn water into ice cubes.

reindeer If your **reindeer** seems droopy, rush him to Alaska. A **reindeer** is a large deer that loves very cold weather. If you ever see **reindeer** up in the sky, get your eyes examined. **Reindeer** can't fly.

remember "I **remember** the day it snowed popcorn," you say. "I was only two years old." When you **remember,** you think about things that happened back there sometime. Can you **remember** what you had for dinner last night?

remove "Kindly **remove** your foot from my foot," says Sandra. Your foot is on her foot, and she would like you to put your foot someplace else. When you **remove** something, you move it from where it is to some other place. Don't **remove** your foot to George's foot. He probably won't like it either.

repeat "I didn't do it. I didn't do it. I didn't do it," you say. If you say something more than one time, you **repeat** it. If you say something you heard someone else say, you **repeat** what he said. **Repeat** just means say again.

request When you **request** something, that means you ask for it. "I **request** a very large tank for my porpoise," you say to your parents. They may say no to your **request.** Probably it would be better if you took your porpoise to the nearest ocean.

rescue Most cities have **rescue** squads trained to get people out of burning buildings or to help people who have been injured. To **rescue** means to get somebody or something out of danger. To **rescue** your cat, you may have to climb a tree and carry the cat down.

rest You get tired from pedaling your bicycle up the steep hill, so you stop for a while to **rest.** When you **rest,** you quit working so hard, and you take time out to breathe easier and get your strength back. Everybody needs to **rest** at times.

restaurant The good thing about a **restaurant** is you don't have to do the cooking or wash the dishes. A **restaurant** is a place where meals are served to anybody who comes in. People bring you whatever food you order. Just remember that you have to pay for what you eat in a **restaurant.**

return "I shall **return** in ten minutes," you say. **Return** means to come back. **Return** also means to give back. If you borrow your friend's bugle and then give it back, you **return** it.

RETURN BUGLES HERE

reward A **reward** is something good that you get for doing a good deed. If you find a leopard in your backyard and return it to the zoo, the zookeeper may give you a **reward.** A **reward** is not always money. If your friend smiles and says, "Thank you," because you were helpful, that is a **reward.**

rhinoceros A **rhinoceros** looks impossible. A **rhinoceros** is a large animal with short legs, thick skin, and a big nose that has one or two horns on it. A **rhinoceros** can't blow its horns. It uses them for fighting. People who know **rhinoceroses** say they have bad tempers.

rib Rub your fingers along the sides of your chest. Those bony things you feel are your **ribs. Ribs** are important. Your **ribs** make a kind of cage that protects your lungs and heart. You have 12 **ribs** on each side of you.

ribbon "Please give me the red **ribbon**," you say. "I need it to tie up this birthday package." **Ribbon** is a thinnish strip of cloth that is used for decoration. **Ribbon** can also mean an honor. If your crow wins the blue **ribbon,** that means he had the loudest voice at the crow show.

rice If you get tired of potatoes, eat **rice.** Millions of people around the world eat **rice** every day. **Rice** is a seed from a kind of grass. So are wheat and corn. **Rice** is grown only in certain parts of the world, because it needs a lot of water and a lot of warm weather.

ride "It feels bumpy when you **ride** a camel," you tell your friend. When you **ride** something, you sit on it or in it, and it carries you someplace. If you **ride** in an airplane, you get there much faster than if you **ride** on a camel.

294

right "I think it's **right** that we should give
Mr. Adam's hat back to him," you say. You
and your friend found Mr. Adam's hat.
A thing that is **right** is fair or legal or
both. **Right** is also a direction. "Turn
right at the next corner." That means
in the direction of your **right** hand.

ring A **ring** is a round thing that
goes on your finger, and a **ring** is
a noise your telephone makes when
someone calls you. There's a circus
ring and a **ringing** sound a bell makes.
There are really two words that we
call **ring.** One means a round thing,
and the other means a sound.

ripe "I'm not sure this apple is **ripe,**"
you say. **Ripe** means fully grown and ready
to eat — if it's an apple. Some apples have
green skins when they are **ripe.** Some
other apples with green skins are **unripe.**
They have to hang on the tree a while longer
to turn yellow or red before they are **ripe.**

river A **river** is a lot of water that keeps moving along like a road from one place to another. Most **rivers** end up at an ocean. You're lucky if you have a **river** near you. You can swim or fish or go boating in a **river.** Keep your **river** clean.

road "Where do you think this **road** goes?" you ask. "I think it goes to Peoria," your friend says. A **road** is a thing for cars and trucks and buses to travel on. Look for a **road** sign. Maybe that **road** goes to Altoona.

robin People in the north are always glad when they see **robins** come back. **Robins** are a sign that spring is coming. **Robins** fly away when the weather turns cold, and they don't come back till the weather turns warm again. Ask a **robin** why he likes to eat worms.

rock Usually people mean a large stone when they say **rock.** But sometimes **rock** is used to mean a kind of music. Also, **rock** can mean what you do when you go back and forth in a **rocking** chair.

roll A ball **rolls** and the wheels on a skateboard **roll.** A thing that **rolls** moves along by turning round and round. A bike with square wheels would not **roll** very well. There is a smallish, round kind of bread called a **roll.** It's not polite to **roll** a **roll.**

roof A bird probably knows more about your **roof** than you do. A **roof** is the top part of the building you live in. If you live in an apartment building, you may never have seen your **roof.** A **roof** keeps the rain off you. Ask a bird what your **roof** looks like.

room "This is my **room**," you tell your friend. That **room** is a piece of space in your home that belongs to you, and maybe to your brother or sister also. You need a lot of **room** to fly a kite, but that kind of **room** doesn't have a door.

rooster A **rooster** is a very noisy chicken. A **rooster** is a male chicken. **Roosters** have a habit of yelling, "Cock-a-doodle-doo," or something like that, when the sun comes up. This habit is very annoying to some people.

root The part of a plant that is in the ground is its **root**. **Roots** are very important. **Roots** bring in water and food for a plant. You eat some **roots**. A carrot is a **root**.

rough "Ouch! That sandpaper is **rough,**" you say. You accidentally fell in the sandpaper bin. A thing that is **rough** has hard, sharp bumps on it that can scratch. Next time, fall into the satin bin. That's soft and smooth.

round A wheel, a ball, and a piece of spaghetti are **round.** A thing that is **round** has a shape like a circle. A **round** thing has no corners. A **round** thing will roll. You will discover that if you try to eat peas with a knife.

rubber **Rubber** is unusual stuff. It can stretch way out and then snap back. It can bend any which way and then come back to its original shape. **Rubber** is used to make tires, erasers, and toys. **Rubber** is made from the sap of a **rubber** tree. A **rubber** band is not a musical group.

rug "Why are you sleeping on the **rug?**" asks your friend. A **rug** is a thing made of cloth that is meant to be put on a floor. A **rug** is softer than a wood or cement floor. Some **rugs** are made by hand and are treasured as much as valuable paintings.

rule You have to understand the **rules** of baseball if you want to play in a baseball game. **Rules** are ways you are supposed to behave. There was a **rule** that Mary couldn't bring her lamb to school. Your school may have the same **rule.**

run When you **run,** you move your feet much faster than when you walk. When you **run,** you get to places much quicker than when you walk. **Running** is good exercise. Try to become a good **runner.**

abcdefghijklmnopqr**s**tuvwxyz

safe You got up that tree before the bear got to you, and now you are **safe.** When you are **safe,** you are protected from harm or danger. A **safe** is also a heavy iron box that money and jewels are kept in to keep them **safe** from robbers.

salt "Pass the **salt,** please," you say. **Salt** has a taste that can only be called **salty,** because it doesn't taste like anything else but **salt. Salt** goes great with meat or baked potatoes, but it tastes terrible on chocolate cake or ice cream.

same "Those two goldfish look the **same** to me," you say. They look exactly alike. They are the **same** size, the **same** color, and the **same** everything. Things that are exactly like each other are the **same.**

sand Sand is rough, gritty stuff you find on beaches. If you hang around deserts, you have seen lots of **sand.** When **sand** is heated so hot that it melts, it turns into glass. The windows in your home started out as **sand.**

sandwich Bread is on both sides of a **sandwich.** In between is stuff like peanut butter and jelly, meat, cheese, egg salad, or lettuce and tomato. Hardly anyone ever makes a soup **sandwich.** A soup **sandwich** gets soggy.

satisfy Satisfy means to do something nice that makes somebody happy. If you clean up the fishbowl as your parents asked you to, that will **satisfy** them. After you eat a big meal, you can't eat another bite. Your hunger is **satisfied.**

saucer A **saucer** is a smallish dish that goes underneath a cup. When you lift your cup, your **saucer** does not fly away. Some people believe they have seen spaceships that are shaped like **saucers** flying in the air. Nobody has really proved that flying **saucers** are real.

save "Help!" your friend yells. He's in water over his head, and he wants you to **save** him. When you **save** someone, you get him or her out of danger. When you **save** money, you put it in a safe place, and you keep on **saving** until you have enough money to buy a steamship.

saw "This **saw** is rusty," you say. It's hard to cut a log with an old, rusty **saw**. A **saw** is a thin metal thing with teeth on it to cut through hard things. **Saw** is also the word you use for see after it is all over.

say When you **say,** you make words come out of your mouth. You can **say** things like "I'm so glad to see you," or "My name is Henry Hoot." The words you **say** become the words you **said** after you **say** them. "I can't believe what you're **saying**," **says** your friend. "I can't believe your name is Henry Hoot."

scare If friends tell you there are ghosts in that house, that might **scare** you. When you are **scared,** things may not be as **scary** as they seem. Tell those ghosts to move out, if you can find them.

school "I have to go to **school** today," you say. A **school** is a building with teachers in it who are supposed to help you learn things. You learn lots of things before you ever go to **school.** You can think of the whole world as a **school** where you can learn all the time.

scissors One **scissor** is no good at all. **Scissors** are two cutting edges like knives that are hooked together. When you squeeze **scissors** together, they can cut paper, cloth, plastic, or even thin iron. Another word for **scissors** is shears.

scratch You know when you have to **scratch.** You itch, and you reach over there with your fingernails and you **scratch.** A **scratch** is also a tiny cut in your skin that you might get from a rosebush. Put a bandage on your **scratch.**

scream Don't **scream** unless you are really in trouble. If a giant crab grabs your toe, it's okay to **scream.** Your **scream** may not make the crab let go, but it may bring people to help you. A **scream** is a loud, long yell.

sea If you go to see the **sea,** you may find **seashells** on the **seashore. Sea** is another word for ocean. Most of our world is covered with **seas.** All of the **seas** are salty.

seal If you could learn to swim like a **seal,** you could win any swimming race. Unless, of course, you tried to race against a real **seal.** A **seal** is a mammal that has learned to live in water. If you and a **seal** raced on land, you would be sure to win.

search When you **search** for something, you hunt for it, and you keep hunting until you find it. If you are **searching** for the missing diamond, you turn over every rock until you find that diamond. Seek is another word that means the same as **search.**

season There are spring, summer, autumn, and winter. These are called **seasons.** In most parts of the world, the weather slowly changes as the **seasons** change. **Season** also means to add salt and spice to food to make it taste better.

SPRING SUMMER

AUTUMN WINTER

seat Be sure you have a **seat** under you when you sit. Otherwise you will fall on the floor. A **seat** can be a chair, a bench, a stool, or even a big rock. The part of you that sits on a chair is sometimes called your **seat.**

second If you ride your horse in a race and one horse is ahead of you as you go across the finish line, you are **second.** There is another word **second** that means a short amount of time. If your horse had been a **second** sooner in crossing the finish line, you might have won first prize.

FINISH

308

secret "I know a **secret,**" you say. "What is it?" asks your friend. If you tell her, it's not a **secret,** because now she knows. The **secret** is that there is a hamster under your hat. If the hamster moves, maybe your friend will guess what the **secret** is.

see "I can **see** all the way from here to Kansas," says Ken. **See** is what your eyes do for you. They take in light and send pictures to your brain. There has to be light for your eyes to be able to **see.** Your eyes cannot **see** in the dark.

seed A tiny **seed** can grow to be a radish, a rosebush, or a giant tree. A **seed** is a thing that starts a new plant growing after you put it in dirt and water it. The nice thing about **seeds** is that you always know what you get. If you plant carrot **seeds,** you get carrots and not cabbages.

seem "That lamb doesn't **seem** right to me," you say. You have never seen a purple lamb before. Maybe that lamb **seems** to be purple because someone poured grape juice on it. A thing may not really be what it **seems** to be. If you wash the grape juice off the lamb, maybe you will find that the lamb is really green.

seldom "I **seldom** put mustard on apple pie," Patty says. **Seldom** means almost never. If you **seldom** go ice skating in July, that means you don't often go ice skating in July. Try January.

selfish "I'm not going to share my pickled mushrooms with anybody," says that kid. That kid is **selfish.** A person who is **selfish** thinks mostly about himself, and he doesn't really care much about other people.

sell When you **sell** something, you give it to somebody, and that person gives you money for it. You don't have to **sell** something that belongs to you if you don't want to. If someone says, "I'll pay you a dime for that dog," you can say, "No, thank you, this dog is not for **sale.**"

send "I'm going to **send** this saddle to Aunt Sally," you say. When you **send** the saddle to Aunt Sally, you don't take it to her yourself, because she lives in Australia. When you **send** something, you count on other people to make sure it gets there.

separate If you are eating jelly beans and you want to save the red ones till last because they are your favorite, you **separate** them. When you **separate** things, you sort them out. To **separate** means to move things apart.

serious There are times when your mother or father asks you to quit laughing and be **serious.** That means there is something important to talk about. Something that is **serious** is something that should be thought about carefully. There are times when it is right to be **serious.**

serve When you put the peanut butter ice cream and grape juice on the table in front of your friends, you **serve** them. To **serve** means to work for somebody, and to help somebody. Anyone who helps you, **serves** you.

set A **set** of dishes is a bunch of dishes that look like they all belong together. When you **set** the table, you put a plate and a knife, fork, and spoon at each place. **Set** often means a group of things, or to put things in a certain place. Please **set** the table with the new **set** of dishes.

seven   If you could teach **seven** toads to sing together, you could probably get that act on a TV show. **Seven** is a number that is one more than six. **Seven** is the number of days in a week. The numeral for **seven** is 7.

several   "I have **several** skunks," you say. **Several** is a loose kind of word that floats around and doesn't mean anything exactly. **Several** means more than two, but probably less than ten. Count those skunks and find out how many you have.

sew   If you know how to **sew,** you can make your own raincoat. When you **sew,** you use a needle and thread to fasten two pieces of cloth or leather or rubber or something together. A **sewing** machine makes the job go faster.

313

shadow "It's not true that Tom is so thin that he has to stand sideways to make a **shadow,**" you say. Anything the sun or a light bulb can't shine through makes a **shadow.** The shade under a tree or a parasol is a **shadow.**

shallow "I like the **shallow** part of the pool," your friend says. Your friend hasn't learned to swim well yet, and he doesn't want to go into the deep part. **Shallow** means not deep. A saucer is **shallow.**

shape A dog has a **shape** that is different from the **shape** of a motorcycle. **Shape** means the outline of the way a thing looks. Even if you can't see one now, you can think of what the **shape** of a tree is.

shark If you don't know whether that **shark** is friendly, it's best not to ask it. Some **sharks** are dangerous and will eat people. Other kinds of **sharks** won't. Most **sharks** are very large fish with lots of teeth in a very big mouth. They hang around oceans, mostly.

sharp ''Be careful! That sword is **sharp,**'' you tell your friend. Your friend is trying to peel potatoes with that sword. A thing that will cut or punch holes easily is **sharp.** A knife and a needle are **sharp.**

she **She** is a word that is used to mean a female creature. You can use **she** to mean your mother, a sister, an aunt, a grandmother, or a female dog or cat. When you are talking about your mother, you are talking about **her.** A thing that belongs to **her** is **hers.**

shell To eat a peanut, you have to crack the **shell**. A **shell** is like a hard overcoat that covers nuts, snails, coconuts, and other such things. A **shell** is a hard outside covering. You don't have a **shell**.

shin The front part of your leg below your knee is your **shin**. You know when you bang your **shin** against a giraffe. That hurts. You probably didn't see that giraffe because he is so tall. Your **shin** will feel better in a minute. So will the giraffe's **shin**.

shine A turned-on light bulb **shines,** and new pennies **shine**. A thing that **shines** gives off its own light, or it bounces back light that comes from somewhere else. If you do a good job of polishing that silver pitcher, it will be **shiny**.

ship "My **ship** has a leak," you say.
A **ship** is a very large boat that is built
to travel across an ocean or a very large
lake. **Ships** carry people or things like
cars, wheat, or rocking chairs.
Fix that leak before your **ship** sinks.

shirt "There's a button gone from
my **shirt,**" your father says.
A **shirt** is a cloth thing with sleeves,
and buttons on the front. A **shirt**
covers the top part of you. Maybe
that button rolled under the bed.

shoe "This **shoe** feels okay, but
that **shoe** feels tight," you say.
Shoes are things you usually wear
on your feet. Sometimes you wear
slippers at bedtime. Sandals are
a bit like **shoes,** except that
sandals don't cover the top part
of your foot as **shoes** do.

short You can't tie the donkey to the tree because the rope is too **short.** A thing that is **short** is not very long or not very tall. Since the rope is too **short,** you have to move the tree closer to the donkey, or move the donkey closer to the tree.

shoulder "My **shoulder** hurts," says Sam. Sam should take that bucket of water off his **shoulder,** and put it on the ground. Your **shoulders** are those flattish places on each side of you where your neck ends and your arms begin.

shout If you say something in a very loud voice, your friend will probably tell you, "Stop **shouting!** I can hear you." People **shout** a lot at ball games and things like that. People tend to **shout** when they are very glad or very angry.

318

shove It's usually not considered polite to **shove** someone. When you **shove,** you push. However, if you help **shove** someone's car out of the snow, he will probably be very grateful.

show "**Show** me your new parrot," your friend says. When you **show** something, you let people see it. **Show** also means a movie, a play, a circus, or something else people pay money to see. Teach your parrot to sing "Yankee Doodle," and you can put him in a **show.**

shut A door that is not open is **shut.** **Shut** also means to close, which means about the same thing. When you **shut** something, you close it. That means it is not open anymore. Make sure your fingers are not in the way when you **shut** the refrigerator.

sidewalk It's much easier to roller skate on a **sidewalk** than on the grass. A **sidewalk** is a hard cement strip between the street and the houses. **Sidewalks** are meant for people to walk on. It's okay to roller skate on a **sidewalk,** too.

silent You have to be **silent** when you try to sneak up on that chipmunk. **Silent** means no noise at all. Don't talk. Walk on tiptoe. Don't step on twigs.

similar Things that are **similar** look a lot alike, but they are not exactly alike. Two apartments may look **similar,** except that one has a red door and the other has a green door. Make sure you know which is your door.

sing Singing is what you do when you say words in a musical way. When you **sing,** you make your voice go up or down when the sound of the music goes higher or lower. If you do a good job, people will appreciate the **song** you **sang.**

sink You put water in the **sink** when it's time to wash the dishes. **Sink** is also what your rowboat does if it gets too full of water. Your rowboat goes down. "My beautiful red rowboat **sank,**" you say.

sit Your dove **sits** on her eggs to make them hatch. You can **sit** on a stool and watch your dove **sitting** on the eggs. When you **sit,** the top part of you is straight up and down, and the bottom part of you is on a chair or a bench or something like that. Don't **sit** on your dove's eggs.

six Six crows yelling "CAW!" at the same time can make an awful racket. **Six** is one more than five, but it is one less than seven. If you can get one of those **six** crows to be quiet, the noise won't be so bad. The numeral that stands for **six** is 6.

skin Your **skin** is marvelous stuff. If it gets cut or scratched, it fixes itself. **Skin** is the outer covering of you before you put on clothes. Your **skin** helps hold you together, and it keeps the rain and the dirt away from your insides.

skunk "Why do people run away from me when they see my **skunk?**" you ask. **Skunks** have a bad reputation. A **skunk** is a smallish animal, about the size of a cat, but it can make a very big stink. It sprays that nasty smell to protect itself, because a **skunk** is actually a very gentle animal.

sky Up there, way over your head, is where the **sky** is. The color of the **sky** is always changing. Sometimes it's blue, sometimes it's orange or rosy, and at night it's black.

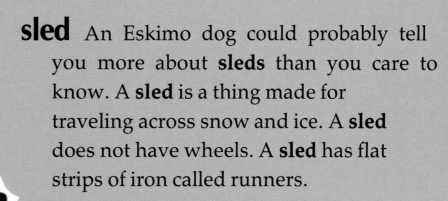

sled An Eskimo dog could probably tell you more about **sleds** than you care to know. A **sled** is a thing made for traveling across snow and ice. A **sled** does not have wheels. A **sled** has flat strips of iron called runners.

sleep "Be quiet; the baby is **sleeping,**" you tell your friend. When a person or an animal **sleeps,** it usually lies down, closes its eyes, and goes into a deep kind of rest. You don't know what's going on around you when you **sleep,** but a loud noise can wake you out of your **sleep.**

323

slow If you want to know about **slow,** ask a snail. Or, you could sit and watch an iron fence rust. A thing that is **slow** takes a long time to get from here to there, or it takes a long time to happen. It may take years for that iron fence to get rusty.

small It's hard to reach that cupboard where the cookies are if you're **small. Small** is another word for little. You won't be **small** all your life. You will get bigger, and it will be easy for you to reach that cupboard..

smell "I **smell** bacon," you say. **Smell** is one of the things your nose does for you. You breathe through your nose, but at the same time your nose tells you what things **smell** like. Bacon has a **smell** that is different from a rose or a piece of cheese.

smile When your mouth turns up at both ends, that's called a **smile.** A **smile** is a sign that you're happy. A **smile** can be a friendly greeting. When you **smile,** people **smile** back at you.

snail Try to imagine what it would be like to carry your house around with you every place you went. That's what a **snail** has to do. And a **snail** only has one foot. Never make fun of a **snail.** Think of the problems it has to put up with.

snake A **snake** is even worse off than a snail. A **snake** has no feet. **Snakes** are longish, round creatures that have to wiggle to get to where they want to go. Maybe you could teach your **snake** to grow wheels.

sneeze "AH-CHOOO!" or something like that, is what you say when you **sneeze.** When you get that tickly feeling in your nose, you can't stop yourself. You **sneeze.** Just remember to cover your mouth when you have to **sneeze.**

snow When the weather is cold and soft, white things fall from the sky, it is **snowing. Snow** is tiny drops of water that freeze before they get to the ground. The amazing thing is that if you look at a million **snowflakes** through a microscope, no two of them look exactly alike.

soap "This **soap** is slippery," you say. The bar of **soap** popped out of your hands. **Soap** is made of fats and chemicals mixed together. It can be used to clean you, the floor, dishes, dirty blue jeans, and other things. **Soap** can be made into a shape, or it can be a powder or a liquid.

socks Most everybody knows that you do not put your **socks** on over your shoes. You put your **socks** on your feet before you put your shoes on. A **sock** is a cloth thing that covers your foot and part of your leg. There is another word **sock** that means to punch somebody. If you do it, he'll probably **sock** you back.

soft "Wow! This is **soft**," you say. There is a pile of feathers on the floor, and you decided to lie on it. Something that is **soft** is smooth or fluffy, and it bends easily. **Soft** means not hard.

some When you say, "Give me **some** baked beans, please," you are not asking for 87 or 103 baked beans. You just want **some**. **Some** means no particular number. The opposite of **some** is none. If you don't have **some,** you have none.

son If you are a boy, you are a **son**. A **son** is a male offspring of two parents. If you become the parent of a boy after you grow up, that boy will be your **son**.

soon "I hope the rest of the family gets home **soon**," you say. You are hungry, and you are waiting for the rest of the family to get home so you can eat. **Soon** means not long from now.

sorry If you feel bad because you knocked your little brother into the mud puddle, you feel **sorry**. When you feel **sorry,** you don't feel happy. It might be because of something you did, or it might not. You are **sorry** it rained on the day you hoped to go on a picnic.

sound Sound is anything you can hear. Sound is waves in the air your eyes can't see but your ears can hear. **Sound** is music, talking, noise, or even a telephone ringing. The invisible **sound** waves of that ringing telephone reach your ears.

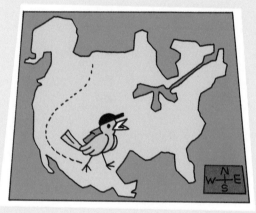

south On most maps, **south** is at the bottom, and north is at the top. In North America, places in the **south** are warmer than places in the north. Robins go **south** when winter comes. A robin can tell you about the **south.**

spider A **spider** may look like an insect, but it's different. A **spider** has eight legs, but an insect has only six. **Spiders** spin webs that catch insects like flies. **Spiders** eat the insects. A **spider** is much quieter than a flyswatter.

329

spoon "It will take a long time to fill this bucket with a **spoon**," you say. A **spoon** is a shallow thing with a handle that you often use when you eat. A **spoon** is mouth-sized, not bucket-sized.

spring A **spring** is a coil of wire that makes a jack-in-the-box pop up. **Spring** is also a time of year when plants pop out of the ground and leaves pop out of trees. They don't really pop, but it seems like it. **Spring** is the time of year when things start growing again.

squirrel If you could do the kind of things a **squirrel** can do, you would be a champion athlete. A **squirrel** can walk on a wire, climb up a brick wall, and jump from branch to branch in a tree. A **squirrel** has a big, bushy tail that helps him do those things. You don't have a bushy tail.

star Those small things you see shining in the sky at night are called **stars.** Those **stars** may look small, but that is because they are so far away. Many of them are much bigger than our sun. **Stars** do not have five points. They are round like our sun.

start When the curtain goes up, the show **starts.** To **start** means the same as to begin. Shows **start,** races **start,** and ball games **start.** After a while, they end.

stay "Why don't we **stay** here tonight?" you say. That leaky old motel doesn't look very good, but you want to **stay** someplace. You are tired of traveling. When you **stay,** you quit moving and stop in one place for a while.

stick You can **stick** with glue, and you can **stick** with a pin or a tack. When you put a stamp on an envelope, you lick the glue side and **stick** it on the envelope. You **stick** a piece of paper on the wall with a tack or some kind of **sticky** tape. A **stick** is also a long, skinny piece of wood that comes from a tree or a bush.

stomach Your **stomach** is where the food goes after you swallow it. A **stomach** is a sort of bag in the middle of you. In your **stomach,** food gets turned into chemicals and things that make your body work. Pity the poor cow with a **stomachache.** A cow has four **stomachs.**

stone "This **stone** is hard to chew," you say. No wonder. A **stone** is a small rock. A **stone** is made of the same kinds of stuff a rock is made of. All these different kinds of stuff are hard.

stop Stop is a short, sharp word that means quit what you are doing. If you are chasing a panther and someone yells, "**Stop!**" that means quit chasing that panther. When the traffic light at a corner turns red, that means **stop.** Don't cross the street till the light turns green.

store When you want to buy a hen or a lizard or a piece of licorice, you go to a **store.** A **store** is a place where things are sold. Another word for **store** is shop. A **storehouse** is a place where things are kept until they are needed.

storm Lightning flashing, thunder crashing, and a strong wind blowing are a **storm.** There is usually rain or snow with a **storm,** too. Nobody has to tell you to get inside when it's **stormy.**

story A **story** is a telling about something. Maybe it really happened, or maybe it's a make-believe **story.** A campfire is a great place for telling **stories.** You could tell the **story** of the time you rode on a flying carpet.

street "I live on Raspberry **Street,**" you say. You don't really live on the **street.** You live in a house that is alongside a **street** named Raspberry. A **street** is a place for cars, trucks, and buses to travel. Sidewalks are on each side of the **street,** and then there are houses and other buildings.

string String is long, thin stuff you can use to fly a kite with or to tie a package with. **String** is thinner and weaker than rope, but it's thicker and stronger than thread.

strong If you can lift heavy weights, you are **strong. Strong** means you have a lot of muscle power, which is also called **strength.** Be careful that you don't drop those weights on your foot.

sudden "All of a **sudden** I met this three-foot-tall guinea pig," you say. A thing that is **sudden** is something you don't expect and that happens fast. "I got to the corner," you say, "and **suddenly** he was there."

sugar It's hard to tell **sugar** from salt just by looking at them. If you taste them, you can tell right away which is **sugar. Sugar** is sweet. Most **sugar** is white and looks like salt, but there is also brown **sugar** and powdered **sugar.**

summer Most people say **summer** is their favorite time of year. **Summer** is the time when plants grow, when trees are green, and when families take vacation trips. **Summer** is the time to be outdoors. **Summer** is a time to goof off.

sun You know when the **sun** is shining. The **sun** is up in the sky, big and round, and so bright you can't look at it. The **sun** warms you, and tans you, and makes things grow. Our **sun** is a star, but it looks bigger and brighter than any other star, because it is so much nearer. Our **sun** is only 93 million miles away.

supper What some people call dinner, other people call **supper. Supper** is the last meal of the day. For many families, it is the only time when everybody can be together.

surprise If a clown suddenly appeared in your living room with a pizza in his hands, that would be a **surprise.** A **surprise** is something you don't expect. When a person is **surprised,** his face usually shows it.

swan If you had a neck like a **swan,** you could look around corners. A **swan** is a big bird with a very long neck that can turn in any direction. **Swans** like to live around ponds and other watery places.

sweater When the weather is chilly but not really cold, you can wear a **sweater.** A **sweater** has sleeves, and it covers the top part of your body, except for your head. If the weather warms up and you start to **sweat,** you can take your **sweater** off.

337

sweet Hamburger that tastes **sweet** wouldn't seem right to most people. **Sweet** is a taste that belongs to things like candy, cake, ice cream, and popsicles. Sauerkraut is not **sweet**. It is sour.

swim An otter could teach you a lot about how to **swim.** He knows how to stay afloat and move around in the water. If you could understand otter talk, you could probably become a great **swimmer.**

swing "I fell off the **swing,**" says Helen. Tell Helen to duck before that **swing swings** back and hits her on the head. A **swing** is a thing to ride on, and **swing** is what it does. **Swing** means move back and forth like the pendulum of a clock.

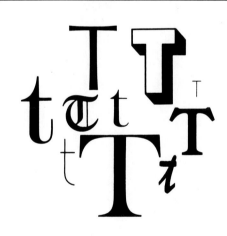

abcdefghijklmnopqrstuvwxyz

table You can put all kinds of things on a **table**. A fishbowl, a horseshoe, a coconut, and a book will all fit on a **table**. A **table** has legs and a flat top to put things on.

tail Most animals have **tails**. **Tail** means the back end of an animal, but usually people mean the longish thing growing on the back end when they say **tail**. The kangaroo is probably the champion **tail** grower. The dog is probably the champion **tail** wagger.

take When you **take** a banana from the fruit bowl, the banana belongs to you. **Take** has a lot of meanings, but mostly it means to make something yours. It's okay if you **took** the banana because somebody offered it to you.

talk "May I **talk**, please," you say. "I would like to tell you how the cat got stuck on the ceiling." When you **talk**, you make words come out of your mouth. **Talk** means the same thing as say.

tall A building that sticks up into the clouds is really **tall**. A thing that is **tall** sticks up higher than most other things of its kind. If you ever see a dog that is eight feet **tall**, you can tell people you have seen a **tall** dog.

tangerine There is no zipper on a **tangerine**, though it often seems that there is. A **tangerine** looks much like an orange, except that most **tangerines** are smaller and more orangish in color than oranges. The skin of a **tangerine** comes off easily.

target "Watch me hit that **target** right in the middle," says Robin. A **target** is a thing you try to hit with something you shoot, like an arrow, or with something you throw. If you hit that **target** with an egg, the **target** will be pretty messy.

taste Even with your eyes closed, you can tell the **taste** of honey. **Taste** is what your tongue does for you. It tells you if a thing **tastes** sweet, sour, salty, bitter, or whatever.

teach You may find it hard to **teach** your camel to dance. When you **teach,** you tell or show somebody something he didn't know until you **taught** him. You don't have to **teach** a squirrel how to climb trees.

342

tear It's easy to **tear** paper, but it's hard to **tear** leather. When you **tear** something, you rip it apart or make a hole in it. There is another word **tear** that has a different meaning and a different sound. That **tear** means the watery stuff that comes from your eyes when you cry.

telephone A **telephone** wire is not a hollow tube. There is electricity in the wire. When you talk into a **telephone,** your voice changes the electricity. At the other end, the electricity is changed back into sound. Your friend can hear what you say.

telescope Our word **telescope** comes from old Greek words that mean seeing far away. A **telescope** is a long thin tube that has lenses in it. With a **telescope** you can see whether that ship way over there is a pirate ship.

temperature   The **temperature** of something is how hot or cold it is. If the **temperature** of the air outdoors is 20 below zero, that is cold. If your parents say you have a **temperature,** they mean your body is hotter than it should be.

ten   Ten is a very important number in our counting system, because we bunch things by **tens.** The numeral for **ten** is 10. That means one bunch of **ten** and no more. The numeral for twenty is 20. That means two bunches of **ten** and no more. You have **ten** fingers and **ten** toes.

thank   "**Thank** you for the electric backscratcher," you say. "It's just what I always wanted." When you **thank** someone, it means you are grateful, or **thankful,** for something that person has given you or done for you.

that "Look at **that**!" says your friend. She has never seen a donkey on roller skates before. **That** means a certain one. She means **that** donkey with the roller skates, and not the others.

theater, theatre* You usually have to hand somebody a ticket when you go into a **theater.** A **theater** is a place where you go to see or hear something, like a movie or a play or a concert.

them **Them** means those people. "I invited **them** to come to my house," you say. I like **them** because they are my friends.

345

there "**There** are six red birds over **there** behind that rock," you say. Usually, **there** means in that place over **there.** Sometimes, when **there** starts a sentence, it doesn't seem to mean anything at all. "**There** may be rain later today," says the man on TV. That **there** doesn't mean anything.

thick A one-foot-high pancake would be called a **thick** pancake. A thing that is **thick** has more stuff from the bottom to the top or from one side to the other than you would expect. You have to be pretty hungry to eat that **thick** pancake.

thin "Come see the **thin** man!" shouts the ticket man at the circus. "He's eight feet tall and weighs 37 pounds." A person like that would be really **thin. Thin** means there is not much between one side and the other side. A piece of paper is **thin.**

thing "How do you work this **thing**?" you ask. **Thing** is a handy word you can use when you don't know the name of it or what it is. A **thing** is **something** that is real, and you can see it. Try pushing that red button.

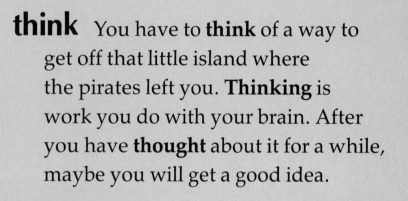

think You have to **think** of a way to get off that little island where the pirates left you. **Thinking** is work you do with your brain. After you have **thought** about it for a while, maybe you will get a good idea.

thirsty A desert is sure to make you **thirsty**. When you are **thirsty**, you have a strong feeling that you want to drink something. Water or lemonade or milk or anything else that's wet will get rid of your **thirst**.

347

this "**This** is my computer," you say. You mean the one you are next to, and not that one over there. When you say **this,** you usually mean the thing closest to you or what you are thinking about. "**This** is what I am going to do," you say.

three If you meet a creature from another planet who has **three** eyes, **three** arms, and **three** toes on each foot, you might think he looks strange. He might think you look strange, because you only have two eyes. **Three** is the number that is one more than two. The numeral for **three** is 3.

throat You only notice your **throat** when it gets sore. Your **throat** is a kind of tube that connects your mouth with your stomach. When you swallow food, it goes down your **throat.**

348

throw   "Watch me **throw** this silver dollar across the river." says George. When you **throw,** you use your hand and your arm. You swing your arm quick and fast, open your hand, and let the thing go rushing through the air.

thumb   Each of your hands has one special finger called a **thumb.** What is so special about a **thumb** is that it is the only finger that can touch its front part to the front part of each of the other fingers on the same hand. Your **thumb** makes it easy to pick things up. Try picking up a dime without using your **thumb.**

thunder   That awful racket you hear during a summer storm is **thunder. Thunder** is noise caused by a flash of lightening. If the lightening is close, the **thunder** may be loud, but it's still only noise. It's all right for your dog to hide under the bed if he is scared of the noise.

tie It's harder to tell someone how to **tie** the laces on a pair of sneakers than it is to do it. When you **tie** something, you fasten it together with a knot. There is a cloth thing called a **tie** that you can wear around your neck.

tiger Be sure to keep your **tiger** well fed. **Tigers** are the biggest cats in the world. **Tigers** are bigger than lions, and they get very mean when they are hungry. They do not eat lettuce. **Tigers** only eat meat.

tight "This collar is too **tight,**" you say. It's smaller than your neck, and you can hardly breathe. You might be in a **tight** situation if your belt and your collar are too **tight.** Get a bigger shirt and belt.

time   A tree stays in one place, but we say **time** moves. A clock tells you what **time** it is right now, but a clock is not **time**. **Time** is an idea. **Time** is the idea that things happened before now, that they are happening now, and that they will happen after now.

to   "I am going **to** the eggbeater shop," you say. Often, **to** means in that direction. "I am going there **to** get my eggbeater fixed." That **to** tells why you are going there. It would take a long time **to** explain all the meanings of **to**.

toad   Don't let people make fun of your **toad**. Your **toad** may look warty and homely, but it is a good friend to people. One **toad** will gobble up thousands of mosquitoes and other bugs. A **toad** doesn't chase bugs; it just sits there. When a bug comes close, zap, the **toad** swallows it.

toast If smoke comes out of the **toaster** and you smell an unpleasant smell, the **toast** is probably getting too **toasty.** Usually, when you say **toast,** you mean bread you heat on both sides till it gets brownish. You can also **toast** a muffin or a marshmallow.

today Whatever day you read this is **today. Today** means this day, right now. Maybe **today** is the day you planned to plant a garden. Do it this day, before **today** becomes yesterday.

toe "It's hard to write with my **toes,**" Terry says. **Toes** stick out from your feet, just as fingers stick out from your hands. But **toes** are not as useful as fingers. Most of the time your **toes** are covered up with socks and shoes.

together If you can get those five sheep into the pen, you will have them **together.** When things are **together,** they are in one bunch. When you and your friends get **together,** you all meet at one place.

tomato A **tomato** is actually a kind of berry. People used to think **tomatoes** were poisonous, but then somebody discovered they weren't. **Tomatoes** taste good raw, cooked, made into juice or ketchup, or made into sauce for pizza.

tomorrow You will never see **tomorrow,** because by the time it comes, it is now today. **Tomorrow** is always the day after this one. When you wake up and try to see **tomorrow,** it has already jumped ahead to the next day.

tongue It's all right to stick
your **tongue** out at your doctor if he
asks you to. Your **tongue** is that flat
thing in the middle of your mouth.
Your **tongue** helps you to talk, and
it tells you how things taste.

tonight "We're going to have
a big campfire **tonight**," you say.
Tonight means this night. **Tonight**
is the last part of today. You
can tell ghost stories around
the campfire **tonight**.

too "There's **too** much soup in my
bowl," you say. That **too** means
there is more soup than your
bowl can hold. Soup is slopping
over the edge. **Too** also means
also. "I have a bowl of soup, and
I have crackers, **too**," says Kate.

tooth Now and then a **tooth** gets loose, and wiggles and itches, and then comes out. Another **tooth** grows in its place. Your **teeth** are much like bones, except that your bones never fall out.

top When you get to the **top** of the stairs, you are as high as you can go. You can't go any higher. The **top** is the highest part of anything. The lid of a jar goes on the **top** of the jar. A hat goes on the **top** of your head.

touch "I can tell that's a cat." Even with a blindfold on, your sense of **touch** tells you it's a cat. **Touch** is a feeling you get from your fingers or from any other part of your body that is **touching** something.

town If you live in a **town,** you live in a place that doesn't have as many people as a city. A **town** does not have tall buildings and crowds of people. **Towns** are nice, quiet places to live in.

toy There are probably hundreds of different kinds of **toys.** A **toy** is anything someone uses for fun or pleasure. Dolls and balls and kites and roller skates are **toys.** A piece of rope is a **toy,** too.

trade "I'll **trade** this doorknob for that glass jar and the tadpole," your friend says. When you **trade,** you give somebody something, and that person gives you something. When you buy something in a store, you **trade.** You give the storekeeper money and **trade** it for the thing you want.

train You may have to run to get on the **train** before it leaves the station. When it's time for a **train** to go, it leaves. A **train** is a bunch of cars hooked together with an engine in front. **Trains** carry people, pigs, potatoes, packages, and many other things.

tree "I planted this **tree**," you say. **Trees** are big plants with woody trunks, branches, and leaves or needles. **Trees** give shade on hot summer days. Some **trees** give fruit. **Trees** are used to make lumber for houses or furniture. Some **trees** get made into paper. **Trees** are great. Plant another **tree**.

trip A **trip** means to go from one place to another place. Probably you and your family have gone on **trips** in the summer or on weekends. When you **trip** over a log, that's a bad **trip**. You go from standing up to lying on your face on the ground.

357

turkey People who grow **turkeys** say that no **turkey** will ever win a prize on a quiz show. A **turkey** is a very large bird, and some people say it is a very dumb bird. Maybe a **turkey** knows a lot more than people think it knows.

turtle A **turtle** never gets a chance to go outdoors. A **turtle** always has to carry its house along wherever it goes. A **turtle** lives its whole life between a top and bottom shell. These shells are called a carapace. A **turtle** doesn't know that, but now you do.

two A pair of slippers is **two** slippers. There is one slipper for your right foot, and one more slipper for your left foot. **Two** is one and one more. Some of the things that come in **twos** are shoes, socks, mittens, and twins. The numeral for **two** is 2.

abcdefghijklmnopqrst**u**vwxyz

umbrella   "I forgot my **umbrella**. Can I get under yours?" your friend asks. An **umbrella** is a cloth and metal or a plastic and metal thing that is meant to keep the rain off you. There is room for your friend under your **umbrella**.

uncle   A brother of your father or mother is your **uncle**, whether you like it or not. You can't choose your **uncles**. They are just there. If you are really lucky, you have an **uncle** who owns an ice cream shop.

under   If you are **under** the bridge, you can't see that goat walking across it. When you are **under** something, you are below it. The thing you are **under** is above you. You are **underneath** it.

understand Understand is a strange word. It doesn't mean you are standing under something. **Understand** means you know something. "I **understand** how that computer works," you say. You know which buttons to push.

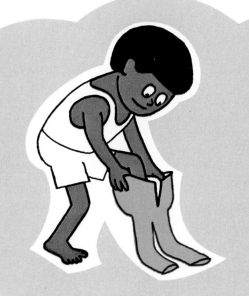

underwear The clothes that go on you under everything else are called **underwear.** There is long **underwear** and short **underwear.** Be sure to get comfortable **underwear,** because it goes right next to your skin.

unexpected You expect a car to travel on a street or a highway. But if your car suddenly started to fly, that would be **unexpected.** A thing that is **unexpected** is something you didn't even dream would happen.

unicorn If you ever see a **unicorn** in your garden, call your nearest zoo. They will be amazed. Ancient writings tell what **unicorns** are supposed to look like, but nobody has ever really seen one. A genuine **unicorn** looks a lot like a horse, but it has one long, twisty horn on its forehead.

uniform A mail carrier looks like a mail carrier because he wears a **uniform**. A **uniform** is a set of clothes that is worn every day by people who do certain kinds of work. The police in your town all wear the same kind of **uniform**.

unique If your squirrel is blue and has red spots, you have a **unique** squirrel. **Unique** means there is nothing else like it in the world. People would like to see your **unique** squirrel. Try to remember where you found it.

unless "I can't paddle this canoe **unless** you give me a paddle," you say. **Unless** means something has to happen first before you can do what you want to do. Even if you get a paddle, you can't paddle that canoe **unless** you pull up the anchor.

untie If you wear sneakers or other kinds of shoes that have laces, you know it's easier to **untie** them than to tie them. When you **untie,** you just grab the two ends and pull. **Untying** a package is the most fun.

up That way  is **up.** **Up** is higher than where you are now. If the balloon you bought at the zoo slips out of your hand, it goes **up.** How high is **up?** Nobody knows for sure.

363

upset "I **upset** that flower pot," you say. When you **upset** something, you don't set it up. You knock it over. That doesn't make much sense, but that is what **upset** often means. Be glad if nobody gets too **upset** because you **upset** the flower pot.

upstairs If you live in a place that has stairs in it, you have an **upstairs.** The **upstairs** is the part you get to after you go up the stairs. The part below you is the downstairs.

use "I know how to **use** this monkey wrench," you say. **Use** means make a thing do what it is supposed to do. Do not try to **use** that monkey wrench on a monkey. That wrench is meant to be **used** to tighten things on machinery and such.

364

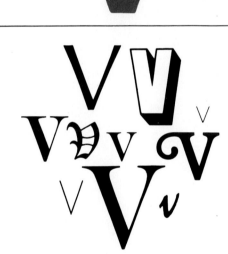

abcdefghijklmnopqrstu v wxyz

vacation Our word **vacation** comes from an old Latin word that means leave. That's what you usually do when you go on **vacation.** You leave. You pack up a bunch of stuff and you go. You can have a **vacation** at home if you don't go to school or do any work.

vacuum A **vacuum** is an empty space where there is nothing, not even air. You make a sort of **vacuum** in your mouth when you suck up a milkshake through a straw. Make sure the family cat is not in the way when you use the **vacuum** cleaner.

valentine Every year on February 14 people send cards to each other that say, "Be my **Valentine.**" Nobody knows exactly what that means or how to be a **valentine.** Mostly, you send **valentine** cards to people you like, and people who like you send you cards.

valley "I live down there in that **valley,**" you say. A **valley** is a low place between hills or mountains. **Valleys** are okay places to live in. Usually a **valley** has a river or a creek. That gives you a place to swim or go fishing.

vanish Your friends can't see the turkey that was on the table, because you made it **vanish.** When a thing **vanishes,** it disappears. When the sun comes out, your snowman will probably **vanish.**

vegetable A **vegetable** just sits there. Day after day it just sits there. Finally, when the **vegetable** gets ripe, you can eat it. A **vegetable** is a plant people eat. Beets, beans, broccoli, corn, cabbage, and carrots are all **vegetables.**

very "I like skiing **very** much," says Mark. **Very** means he likes it a lot. He is **very** happy when he skis. He likes to ski even more than he likes to eat ice cream.

veterinarian If your gnu gets sick, take it to a **veterinarian.** A **veterinarian** is an animal doctor. That doesn't mean a **veterinarian** is an animal that is a doctor. It means a **veterinarian** is a human who tries to fix up sick or hurt animals.

view "The **view** from up here is terrific," you say. From your giant balloon, you can see for miles around. A **view** is what you can see. **View** can also mean what you think. "My **view** is that we should go back down to the ground now."

village A **village** is smaller than a city, and even smaller than a town. Not many people live in a **village.** Usually everybody knows everybody else in a **village.** Some **villages** have strange sounding names like Balls Mills.

violet One sure sign that spring has come is when the **violets** bloom. **Violets** are small flowers that have a **violet** smell and usually a **violet** color. It takes a long time to pick a big bunch of **violets,** but it's worth it.

visit When you **visit** a friend or a place, you only mean to be there for a short time. You don't plan to spend the rest of your life there. When you **visit** a museum, you go there for a while. Then you go home. While you are **visiting,** you are a **visitor.**

voice The sounds that come out of your mouth, whether you are talking, singing, yelling, or whispering, are your **voice.** You're lucky to have a **voice.** Your **voice** lets you talk to people, ask for things, and cheer at ball games.

volcano A **volcano** is a deep hole which goes far down into the earth where everything is very hot. Melted rocks, ashes, and giant stones sometimes come flying out of a **volcano.** It's a good idea to look at a **volcano** from far away.

vote When you **vote,** you raise your hand, say yes or no, or put a piece of paper in a box. When you **vote,** you are saying that you want the person you are **voting** for to be elected. Sometimes you **vote** on whether you think something should or shouldn't be done.

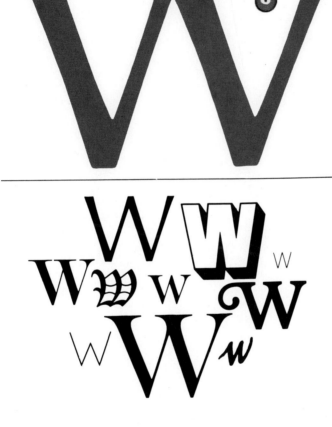

W W W W
W W W W
W W W W

abcdefghijklmnopqrstuvwxyz

walk To **walk,** you put one foot in front of the other foot, then you move the other foot in front of the foot you moved first. You keep on doing this. **Walking** is a slower way of getting there, but it can be more fun. When you **walk** through a forest you see more than if you go through in a car.

wall "I'm going to nail this picture on the **wall,"** you say. An indoor **wall** is an up and down thing that goes from the floor to the ceiling. Outdoor **walls** start from the ground and just go up. Ask your parents if they would like to have that picture of a garbage can on the living room **wall.**

walrus A **walrus** is a large sea animal with long whiskers and big teeth. Many people think **walruses** look funny, but **walruses** don't seem to mind. **Walruses** seem to be pleasant, good-natured animals.

water The wet stuff you wash with, swim in, and drink is called **water.** The surprising thing is that **water** is made of two gases in the air that you can't see. Their names are hydrogen and oxygen. Very hot **water** turns into steam, and very cold **water** becomes ice.

weather "What's the **weather** today?" you ask. The best way to find out is to go outside and feel how the air is and look up at the sky. **Weather** is all about what's going on outdoors. Is it sunny or cloudy or raining? Is it cold or hot or in-between? Is it windy or still? How's your **weather** today?

week Sometimes you hear things on the news like, "This is National Pickle **Week**." The pickle people hope you will eat pickles all **week.** That's a long time. A **week** is seven days. On a calendar, a **week** starts on Sunday and ends on Saturday. There are 52 **weeks** in a year.

west   If you look in the direction where the sun goes down, you are looking **west. West** is the opposite direction from east, where the sun rises. No matter where you go in the world, there is always some place that is **west** of you.

wet   "All of a sudden it started to rain, and I got **wet,**" you say. When you are **wet,** you have water all over you. Your clothes are dripping. **Wet** is **wetter** than just damp. Ask somebody to please get you a dry towel.

whale   If you can train a **whale** to carry you on its back, you can cross oceans in a hurry. Large **whales** are the biggest mammals in the world. Some **whales** are 100 feet long. Take an umbrella along on your **whale** ride. **Whales** spout water.

wheel Nobody will ever know who invented the **wheel.** The **wheel** was invented long before people learned to write. **Wheels** are used today on bikes, cars, trucks, buses, and many other kinds of things. **Wheels** are round. Square **wheels** on a bike would give you a bumpy ride.

whisper You have to get real close to someone if you want him or her to hear your **whisper.** A **whisper** is a very soft and quiet kind of talk. You **whisper** to someone things you don't want other people to hear.

whistle Maybe you have trained your dog to come when you **whistle.** To **whistle,** you have to pucker up your lips in a certain way and blow. If you get good at **whistling,** you can learn to **whistle** tunes.

white Nothing can be **whiter** than **white.** If a thing you are looking at is **white,** it has no color at all. New snow is **white.** So are cotton and fluffy clouds in a blue sky.

wife A **wife** is a woman who is married to a man who is called her husband. A **wife** and a husband are supposed to share things and to help each other.

wind Air that is going places in a hurry is called **wind. Wind** can make a sailboat go, and a stormy **wind** can blow down a tree. There is another word that is spelled the same but has a different sound. You **wind** your clock when it runs down.

winter   If you like to ski or ice skate, you probably love **winter.** If you hate to wear earmuffs and shovel snow, you probably don't like **winter. Winter** is the time of year when the northern part of our world is very cold. People stay indoors mostly during **winter.**

wolf   Be sure to keep your **wolf** on a leash. **Wolves** eat only meat. They will eat rabbits, sheep, moose, and even people. **Wolves** look like dogs, and they are related to dogs. **Wolves** belong in the forest.

woman   A **woman** is a girl who has grown to be an adult. A **woman** has a shape that is different from that of a man. It used to be that **women** wore clothes and had jobs that were different from men, but that is not so true now.

work "I can't talk any longer, because I have to get to **work** now," you say. You promised to mow Mr. Higby's lawn, and he promised to pay you a dollar. **Work** is something you do because it has to get done.

world   Our **world** is a large, round ball, and we are all traveling through space on it. For centuries people thought the **world** was flat like a table and they would fall off the edge if they traveled too far. Our **world** is a planet named Earth.

write   "I would like to **write** a secret message to Patsy, but I don't know how to **write**," says your friend. When you **write**, you put marks on paper that other people can understand are words. Chickens can make marks on paper, but they can't make marks that mean words.

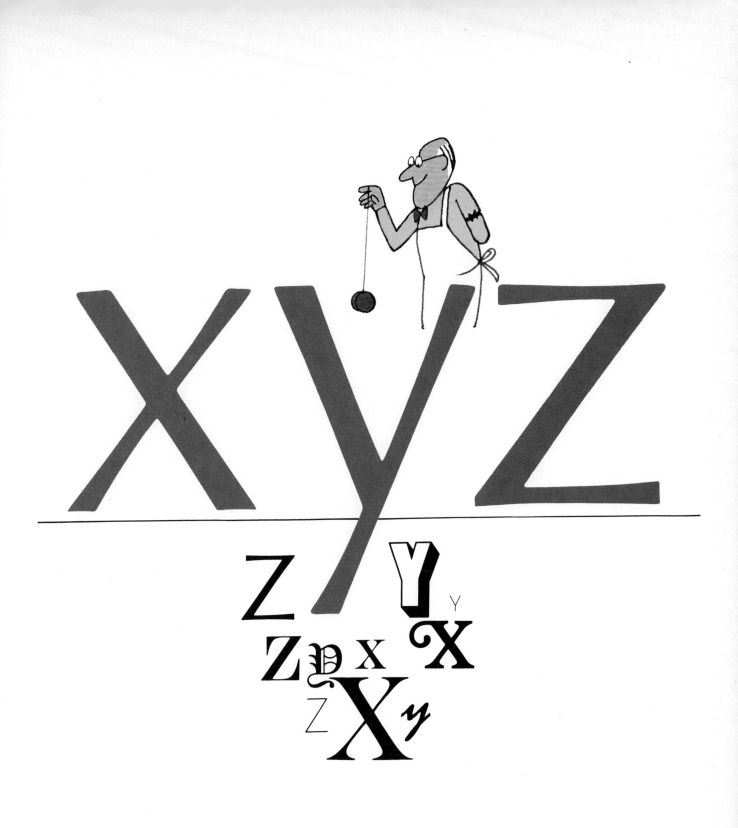

abcdefghijklmnopqrstuvwxyz

x ray   You can't see **x rays,** but they can see right through you. **X rays** were discovered by a man named Roentgen. He called them **x rays** because he didn't know what they were, and he didn't know what else to call them. Doctors use **x rays** to find out what things are like inside your body.

xylophone   To look at a **xylophone,** you wouldn't think it could make music. A **xylophone** looks like a bunch of scraps from a lumberyard. A **xylophone** player hits the pieces of wood with things called mallets. A good player can get beautiful sounds from a **xylophone.**

yak   You are not likely to see a **yak** wandering around town. **Yaks** are big, hairy animals that look a bit like cows. **Yaks** normally live in mountains in Asia. There is another word **yak** that means to talk on and on and on. **Yaks** don't **yak.** They only grunt.

yawn   When somebody **yawns,** it always makes you feel that you want to **yawn,** too. People usually **yawn** when they are sleepy. When you **yawn,** you open your mouth wide, take in a big breath, and let it out. It is not considered polite to **yawn** at your father's jokes.

year   People have parties and shout "Happy New **Year**!" at each other on the night when January 1 starts. That is the time when a new **year** begins. Actually, any time of 12 months is a **year**. The time between your last birthday and your next one is a **year.**

yell   "Please don't **yell** at me," you say. Make sure you are not **yelling** when you say it. When a person **yells,** he talks in a very loud voice. Usually, people **yell** when they are hurt, angry, or happy. A happy **yell** is more pleasant than an angry **yell**.

yellow "I'm wearing my **yellow** sweater, because I'm going to pick daffodils and lemons," your friend says. **Yellow** is a color. It is the color of daffodils, lemons, canaries, grapefruit, and butter. **Yellow** paint and blue paint make green paint. **Yellow** and red make orange.

yes One of the nicest words to hear is **yes. Yes** means your friend agrees with you and will help you put up the tent. **Yes** always means you agree or you think something is true. You don't always have to say **yes.**

yesterday You will never live **yesterday** again. **Yesterday** is always the day before this one. Do something nice today, like teaching a young bird to fly. Tomorrow, when today has become **yesterday,** you can think back and say, "**Yesterday** was a nice day."

you   **You** is always the person being talked to. "Would **you** like to play Ping-Pong with me?" **you** ask. Your friend says, "No, thank **you**." When your friend talks to **you,** **you** are the person who is **you.**

young   A frisky puppy is **young,** and so is a kitten. Any living thing, whether it's a plant or an animal, that is in the early part of its life is **young.** If you are a child, you are **young.** A **young** person is sometimes called a youth.

zebra   A **zebra** looks like a horse wearing striped pajamas. It's hard to decide whether there are white stripes on a black hide or black stripes on a white hide. That has probably never bothered **zebras.** They don't look confused.

zero   Zero is where it all begins. Zero means there is nothing at all, and the numeral for **zero** is 0. If you have no dogs at all, you have **zero** dogs. If you are going on a trip and you haven't left the house yet, you have gone **zero** miles. Beyond **zero,** everything is more.

zoo   You would have to travel all over the world to get to see all the different kinds of animals, birds, and snakes you can see in a **zoo**. A **zoo** is a place where all kinds of creatures are brought together so people can see them. Maybe the polar bear gets as much fun from looking at you as you get from looking at him.

zoom   If you could invent a helicopter helmet, you could **zoom** through the air. A thing that **zooms** moves fast, and it often makes a **zooming** noise. Snails, worms, and turtles never **zoom**.